tough as nails

ONE WOMAN'S JOURNEY THROUGH WEST POINT

Gail O'Sullivan Dwyer

SOMERSET CO. LIBRARY
BRIDGEWATER, N.J. 08807

HELLGATE PRESS   ASHLAND, OREGON

TOUGH AS NAILS

©2009 Gail O'Sullivan Dwyer

Published by Hellgate Press (an imprint of L&R Publishing, LLC)

All rights reserved. No part of this publication may be reproduced or used in any form or by any means, graphic, electronic or mechanical, including photocopying, recording, taping, or information and retrieval systems without written permission of the publisher.

Hellgate Press
PO Box 3531
Ashland, OR 97520

email: info@hellgatepress.com

Editor: Harley B. Patrick
Cover design: L. Redding

Library of Congress Cataloging-in-Publication Data

Dwyer, Gail O'Sullivan.
  Tough as nails : one woman's journey through West Point / Gail O'Sullivan Dwyer ; [editor], Harley B. Patrick. -- 1st ed.
     p. cm.
  Includes bibliographical references and index.
  ISBN 978-1-55571-663-9 (alk. paper)
  1. Dwyer, Gail O'Sullivan. 2. United States Military Academy--Biography. 3. United States. Army--Biography. 4. United States. Army--Women. 5. Women military cadets--United States--Biography. 6. Women soldiers--United States--Biography. I. Patrick, Harley B. II. Title.
  U410.M1D84 2009
  355.0092--dc22
  [B]
                              2009025875

Printed and bound in the United States of America
First edition 10 9 8 7 6 5 4 3 2 1

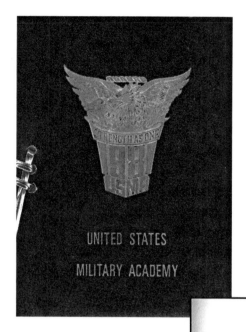

1981 CLASS ROLL

Robert Board Newman
Tracy Lane Newsome
Robert Allen Newton
James Marshall Nichol, Jr.
Brian Jay Nichols
Camille Marie Nichols
Mark Alan Nipper
Duke Naoki Nishimura
George Adelbert Nowak
Robert Masaru Nozuka
Jesse Robert Nutt
Robert Dale Obrien
David Christopher Ochs
Christopher John O'Connell
Edwin Sanderson O'Connor
Francis Gerald O'Connor
Mark Ogara
Gerald Brian O'Keefe
Walter Joseph Olker
Frederick John Ondarza
Cynthia Ann Oneil
Gary Gray Orban
William Dale Osborne
Thomas Sean Oshaughnessy
Alixande C. Osuch
Gail Marie O'Sullivan
Scott Dean Owen
Louis Joseph Pagenine
Mark Alan Palmer
Ralph Matthew Palmiero
Raymond Patrick Palumbo
William Scott Parker
William Henry Parrish
Markian Gregory Pasilwsky
Bonnie Elizabeth Patton
Ross Douglas Pauley

Eugene Pacelli Paulo
John Charles Paulson
James Michael Pawlak
Robert Andrew Payne
Ronald Lee Pearson
William Charles Peck
Stephen Michael Pelicano
David Robert Pelizzon
Philip Walter Pellette
Steven Patrick Perry
Thomas Jay Perry
Scott Christopher Peters
Darryl Wayne Peterson
Jeffrey Neal Peterson
Janet Elizabeth Petro
James Echol Petty, Jr.
Charles Edward Phillips, Jr.
John Thomas Phillips
Dana James Fillian Pittard
Debra Lynn Pittman
Brian David Plaisted
Mark Bennett Pilakos
Andras Huan Ploompuu
Russell Lee Poling
Anita Mukne Polite
Randolph Wayne Ponder
Edward Michael Poniatowski
Ronald Anthony Potter
Elizabeth Ruth Potter
Kenneth Wayne Powell
Robert Howard Pozsonyi
William Joseph Prantl
Richard Brent Pridgen
John Joseph Prusiecki, Jr.
Harvey Leroy Pullen
David Patrick Pursell

Graduation ceremony program,
West Point Class of 1981

To the Long Gray Line and the families that sustain it...

E'er may that line of gray
Increase from day to day;
Live, serve, and die, we pray,
West Point for thee...

contents

Alma Mater

Hail, Alma Mater, dear!
To us be ever near.
Help us thy motto bear
thru' all the years.
Let Duty be well performed,
Honor be e'er untarn'd,
Country be ever armed,
West Point, by thee!

Guide us, thine own, aright,
Teach us by day, by night,
To keep thine honor bright,
For thee to fight.
When we depart from thee,
Serving on Land or sea,
May we still loyal be,
West Point to thee!

And when our work is done,
Our course on earth is run,
May it be said, "Well done,
Be thou at peace."
E'er may that line of gray
Increase from day to day;
Live, serve, and die, we pray,
West Point, for thee!

-Paul S. Reinecke

*(Text amendments for gender
inclusion made in June 2008)*

author's note

My mother used to say, "Honey, if you don't have anything nice to say, don't say anything at all."

If I didn't have anything nice to say and it wasn't important to the story, I didn't say it. If I didn't have anything nice to say and it made the story what it was, then I changed the name. If you're reading this and think you might be a character whose name was changed, maybe you should consider not doing things that aren't nice.

The conversations cited are not verbatim, but were composed from memory based upon the situation.

All other parts of this story are as I remember them, as I perceived them.

There are women who have gone to West Point who did not have positive experiences and I regret that. I only wish all had a story such as mine.

One final thought: I didn't do anything; I realize that. I was offered an opportunity to be a part of history; I took it. We all have a story. I just wrote mine down.

This is my story.

prologue

My husband was naked when we met. Or so he says.

He tells the story more than I care to hear and I always interrupt, scoff, deny, rebut. But, I think people really believe him. People just like to believe weird stuff. That's why they buy magazines with stories of aliens and Elvis on Maui.

He didn't have a shirt on. I'll give him that. He was sitting on his bed in his barracks room at West Point, playing a guitar and the guitar covered his lap, which covered his major male body part. It was that kind of hot that suffocates everything except the New York gnats. The barracks weren't air conditioned. We didn't even have fans.

We were both cadets at the United States Military Academy at West Point. It was the summer before his senior year and my junior year. He was in the Class of 1980, the first class that admitted women, and I was a member of the Class of 1981, the second class with women. (We all knew we weren't nearly as important as the first.)

I'd met his roommate earlier in the day and that's who I was looking for. Instead, I found this guy, sitting on his bed playing the guitar without a shirt on. I thought to myself: The last thing I'd do on a stifling, miserable day is play the guitar naked on my bed. Then I thought something else to myself: The *other* last thing I'd do is be attracted to a guy who played the guitar naked on his bed.

So, the weird part of this story is that we've been married now for over twenty-eight years.

There are people who ask me, "How could you not see that he was naked?"

These people don't know me well. I miss stuff like that all the time. I live in my own little world, oblivious to realities that don't match my perceptions. Where I came from, naked men didn't sit on beds playing the guitar. Where I came from, naked men didn't sit anywhere. There weren't any

Gail O'Sullivan at 8 months. Bonnet later replaced by grey mailman hat. Sept. 1959

naked men where I came from. If I'd said the word "penis" in front of my mother, she'd have had a heart attack and died on the spot. So why would I expect there to be one, a bare one, beneath that guitar? I didn't. I didn't see a naked guy on that bed; I saw a guy with gym shorts on.

Don't we all see what we want to see, how we want to see it? When I left Braintree, Massachusetts in July of 1977 to go to West Point, I saw an opportunity. It was an opportunity that I didn't rightfully deserve, but just because I happened to be at the right place at the right time in history, it was given to me. It was a gift. And I accepted the gift the way I was brought up, politely, apologetically, trying to prove that I deserved it. Sure, I saw bitterness and I saw injustice. I accepted this, too, the way I was brought up, patiently, gently, feeling bad about it. I saw myself breaking down the walls of prejudice one brick, one cadet, one instructor, one old grad at a time. That's what I saw. That's all I saw.

Sometimes I missed stuff that was standing smack dab in front of my eyes because I was too busy earning that gift, too busy fulfilling dreams. Sometimes seeing what you want to see isn't such a bad idea. If I'd seen that penis under the guitar, I'd have crawled out of that room and away from that guy, away from the road I've been on for the past thirty years. Sometimes, when you miss stuff, you have the best time of all.

Gail in 3rd grade

one

Impossible Dreams

I felt like I was waiting in line for the roller coaster at Paragon Park. If I did roller coasters, that is. I don't even do Ferris wheels. But, if I did, I would have that same belly-lurching, I'm-going-to-throw-up sensation that overtook me that April morning in fifth grade. I wanted to do it, but was scared to death.

Nuns could do that to you. I'd never said more than boo, a hushed "Good morning, Sister" to a nun before. We didn't talk to nuns. We didn't even look at them. Eye contact only meant trouble; conversation was never good.

And there I was: Eleven years old, long brown braids tied with navy blue ribbons that matched my navy blue jumper with SFA embroidered on the front right pocket. I was waiting to initiate a real conversation with Sister Agnesca, the strictest, meanest nun at St. Francis of Assisi Grammar School. Armed only with her stare, she could have convinced Charles Manson to join the Peace Corps.

The bell rang. It was a manual bell, brass with a black handle, rung in the hallway by a chosen eighth grader, every forty-five minutes, then placed back on the tile floor between the seventh and eighth grade classrooms. The other fifth graders filed out of the classroom by rows. The desks in Sister Agnesca's class never moved: Four rows of ten desks, lined up neatly in formation. I got up slowly from my desk, fighting back the impulse to just follow my best friend Sharon Preziosi right down the aisle and into the hallway. I wanted to tell this woman, this ancient nun who stopped class when the clock struck the hour, in the middle of the lesson, no matter what it was, and sang a blessing to thank God for the new hour.

I walked up to her slowly as she erased the board. I touched the rope belt that hung down the creases of the long black habit. I gave the rope a slight yank. I couldn't see much of her face. Nuns traveled incognito. We wondered what they wore for pajamas but the thought was so not pretty, we didn't wonder long. I looked up at two pink, pocked cheeks and a long scaly nose. Her entire forehead was covered by the big white triangle in the black flowing headpiece. Her upper face was hidden by big, black-rimmed, mannish glasses.

She responded to my yank.

"Yes, Gail?" Was there concern in those little blue eyes?

Concern or no concern, I stood petrified, frozen in place.

She waited. But I knew I didn't have long before her patience was history. The pressure was on; I had to thaw out and say something fast. I did.

"Sister, my brother is going to West Point."

She cocked her head. She didn't say a word, waiting for me to continue. I did have more to say, but it was stuck.

Sister Agnesca finally responded, "Well, that's just wonderful, Gail."

It unstuck and I burped it up. It came out sounding determined, I thought.

"And I'm going to go there too some day!"

After I said it, I cringed with embarrassment. My eyes watered, like they do when I'm sinking in deep emotions. I couldn't believe I said it.

And I couldn't believe Sister Agnesca smiled. She was not what we'd call a "smiler." Her arthritic hands moved to her hips. She leaned down towards me. We locked eyes. She nodded her head so her black headpiece bounced up and down softly and then, she spoke calmly, like I had said nothing to surprise her, "You know, Gail, I do believe you will."

She said I could do it.

The year was 1969, six years before Congress voted to allow women to attend the service academies.

✦ ✦ ✦ ✦

"Two roads diverged in woods,
and I took the one less traveled by.
And that has made all the difference."

— Robert Frost

Ignore me and I'm yours. I don't know why this is true. Some people crave attention; I'm a non-attention craver and always have been. I seek out those who don't give me the time of day. I crave to be loved by those who ignore me best. It may be a result of genetics. My mother loved to be loved; my father didn't know how. Merge the two and out I came, idolizing people who don't know I'm alive.

Author with her brother, Paul, West Point Class of 1974, at an Army football game in 1978

My brother Paul is eight years older than I. He knew I was alive. We sat at the same dinner table and he had to have noticed me there, but I'm not sure if he could have picked me out in a police lineup. I'm not seeing a therapist because of this, just stating a fact. When he was in high school, and I was in grammar school, he couldn't have told you what grade I was in, what my favorite dessert was, what my worst subject was. If he did ask, I doubt he would have made the connection. It was brownies, no nuts, just like his; it was math, just like his.

This arrangement worked out well for me, the non-attention craver. If Paul had sat with me and played Monopoly, I wouldn't have this story to tell.

I was a little groupie in pig-tails. I sat through all his high school gymnastics meets, closing my eyes as he vaulted over the horse and whispering prayers as he flipped handsprings on the mat. When I heard him at home coming down from his bedroom, taking the stairs three at a time, and opening the front door to sky out of the house, I'd charge to the door, pleading, "Where are you going? Huh? Huh? Can I come?"

And my idol always shouted back to me, "Crazy! No!" Then he shut the white wooden front door, leaving me behind.

If he'd let me go with him then, would I have still felt so compelled to follow him years later?

I wasn't even fazed by Paul's inattentiveness. When he was accepted to the United States Military Academy Preparatory School, I bragged about him to anyone who would listen. I had no idea what this place called the prep school was, but such details were irrelevant. The excitement in my parents' voices meant this was a very big deal. I figured it had to be an honor. I popped with pride.

I didn't find out what the U. S. Military Academy Preparatory School—USMAPS or Prep School—was all about until I was in high school myself. A year of intensive math and English study only offered to those candidates whose academic background is considered weak, being offered the prep school is like telling a guy you'll go out with him if he goes to dancing school first. If the prepster, referred to as a cadet candidate, survives the academic rigors of the year, he is offered a slot in the next year's class at West Point. Paul survived his prep school year and was accepted as a member of West Point's Class of 1974.

The first day that a new cadet reports to the United States Military Academy is called R-Day, short for Reception Day. My first visit to West Point was on Paul's R-Day in July 1970. It was boiling hot. My mother made me and my younger brother, Fred, wear matching red, white and blue outfits. (Fred's real name was Gerard, but only my mother called him that. When she brought him home from the hospital, my older brothers decided he looked like Fred Flintstone and the name stuck, with everyone except my mother because that's what a mother does—she calls you by your real name.)

Despite my fascination with West Point and adoration of my brother Paul, I really wanted to stay at the hotel and swim in the pool, a real treat for us. Back home, we normally swam at Sunset Lake, freezing water, zillions of kids and rocks and broken glass. But the overbearing heat was a distant second to my feelings toward those white polyester shirts with the flag-like trim and the red shorts. I was mortified. I was going into sixth grade, way too old to be dressed up like my little brother. I was so mad at my mother that all other events of the day were inconsequential.

Driving Paul to West Point in our white Dodge Colt station wagon was a family vacation for us. We didn't do vacations. We didn't stay in hotels, ever. When we went out to eat, it was a very big deal. Every blue moon, we drove to the Five Corners (only in Massachusetts would five main streets come together at a vertex with only a blinking yellow light to order the chaos) and piled out of the parking lot at the Chinese restaurant. Fred and I shared the pu-pu platter, while my parents ordered their Manhattans and beef chop suey. My father always commented on the cats in the alley behind the restaurant, implying that we were eating their relatives, which didn't do much for my appetite. This was a rare occasion, though. Going out to eat was an extravagance for my depression-era parents; we ate at home.

Luigi's Restaurant in Highland Falls, just beyond the gates of West Point, wasn't much different than eating at home. On the main street of this tired town that looked like it should have had a coal mine supporting it, the restaurant was right off the set of Andy Griffith. Round tables with wooden chairs and family-style dining. Where's Aunt Bea? Still, for us, it was eating out, so a rather big deal.

The night before Paul's R-Day: his last family dinner until Christmas, eating out in a restaurant, a momentous occasion, calling for momentous conversation. I waited for my father to tell his son how proud he was, how he was sure Paul would succeed. I thought my mother might even get emotional, maybe a bit weepy, at her all-grown-up son, leaving to serve God and Nation. Funny, but the only words of wisdom spoken came from my mother when she warned my little brother, "Don't lean back on the chair, Gerard."

As with most of life's words of wisdom, her instructions went unheeded. The chair flew back with my nine-year-old brother in it, crashing to the floor. It was a riot. Paul and I cracked up; my parents didn't. I liked sharing this with Paul, even at the expense of Fred's head which did hit the floor pretty hard.

Don't lean back on the chair, Gerard: Advice for life from parents who care.

We never really talked in our family. The children listened, the adults talked, more to each other, than to us. I was a great eavesdropper. My mother called me "Miss Nosey Britches," and I never missed a conversation that concerned Paul and West Point. I picked up pieces here and there, the quiet observer, the family spy, and concocted an image of West Point in my mind. It was this really neat place and, if you went there, people were very impressed.

West Point was only four hours from our home in Massachusetts and we visited whenever my parents had a good excuse and there was no cards on Saturday night. My parents rotated once a month with the telephone crowd: the Hanlons, Flahertys, McCloskeys, McGowans, and Boyles. The men had all been friends since after the Big One, WW II. They all worked together for New England Tel & Tel, first as linemen or repairing phones, later work-ing their way up to decent supervisory positions, two cars, suburbia, a dou-ble-wide down on the Cape. Cards meant Budweisers, Manhattans, ruffles and French onion soup dip, though occasionally the hostess would come up with something original, usually on Ritz crackers, and my mother would come home with a recipe, scrawled on the back of a piece of scrap paper she had folded neatly and placed in her huge pocketbook.

Paul just wanted to be James Bond. Or James West, from "The Wild, Wild West," a '60s TV show in which suave James always got the bad guy and the va-va-va-voom girl. You never see either of those James's calling their mother. When Paul was a cadet, we never heard from him. He didn't call home to whine, to complain, to beg us to come visit him. When he did call—always collect on a Sunday afternoon—my parents had to dig deep to find out what was going on his life. When you got off the phone with Paul, you won-dered what did he just say. Paul was born with the ability to converse without re-vealing his feelings. Perhaps the visits to West Point were to assure my parents that all was well....Or maybe, they were a just a good excuse to party.

Tailgates were card nights in parking lots. With my brother a cadet, the gang had the perfect excuse to throw tailgate extravaganzas, parties held be-tween Impalas and Dodge Colts, where coolers and card tables loped out from the car trunks. Even the kids got to go. We drank Fanta orange and ate cold roast beef subs and stared at the cadets, who to me were all so god-like, so handsome, and magnetic, strong and polite. I loved the uniforms. I loved the parades. Our visits were on autumn football weekends, with the scenery right out of a tourist pamphlet, and the air crisp. In the sixth grade, I was sold.

Then, about two years after my first tailgate, there was talk in the news about allowing women to attend the service academies. I should have been thrilled. I should have been jumping up and down for joy. But, as a pre-ado-lescent, heavily influenced by the opinions of those whom I loved and tried so hard to please, I wasn't particularly thrilled or ecstatic.

I was wishy-washy.

Opening West Point up to women would ruin the place, said my father and brother, the two main men in my life. They said this with feeling! All would be lost. So much tradition down the drain! I heard their arguments. I felt their pain. I loved West Point, but for the good of the Academy, despite my own longing to be a part of it, I found myself agreeing with my father and brother. Women should not go there.

I was a letter writer at an early age. Sister Dorothea, the liberal nun who first wore a green checkered suit instead of the long black habit, and went by her real name instead of the long-assigned nun name, taught us in fourth grade that we could change the world by writing letters. (She also said there was no Noah, no ark; this sent the parents into a tizzy.) I worried as I heard my father and brother bemoaning their fears that West Point would be ruined by the admittance of women. So, using my best Palmer Penmanship, I wrote a letter to President Nixon. Don't let women into West Point, I wrote. You'll ruin the place. You'll spoil the aura. Open a separate academy just for women somewhere else.

For whatever reasons—growing up in a house of boys, spending the day in a Catholic school, not participating in organized sports, or perhaps simply chromosomal make-up—I was not very assertive. I was a people pleaser. It's why I was put on this earth. People pleasers worry that if they are assertive, people may not be pleased. So, people pleasers back off. People pleasers usually get walked on. People pleasers tend toward wishy-washiness and that's where I was. I wanted to be a part of West Point, but I wasn't sure if women should be there. When Congress voted to allow women into the service academies, I wanted to be a cadet. I wanted it a lot.

I needed to hear what Paul thought. (This sounds much less male-dominated than "needed Paul's approval.") On a Saturday afternoon in February in 1976, my father dialed Ft. Rucker, Alabama. Paul had graduated from West Point, had applied to and was selected for flight school, and was at Ft. Rucker learning how to fly helicopters. All this meant as much to me as prep school had meant seven years earlier. I asked Paul what he thought about Congress's decision. He responded without skipping an Airborne Ranger Infantry Cobra pilot heartbeat, "Women shouldn't go there."

After I hung up, my father asked me what Paul had to say. I told him, "He said women shouldn't go there and I think he's right. I can't apply on principle, Dad."

My father was hard to figure out. I never really tried. I never really talked to him. He had narcolepsy and was asleep most of my childhood. When he was awake, he was either working or emulating Archie Bunker from the TV show, "All in the Family." I knew he loved me, but we never said the love word, so I *guessed* he loved me. I knew he was proud of me, though he never really told me, so I *guessed* he was proud of me. I didn't expect emotion from my father; it was like we excused him from showing emotion because he himself came from such a screwy family. In Webster's, next to "eccentric" is a picture of my father's father, whom I barely remember, the infamous J. J. O'Sullivan.

J. J. wore a beanie on his Gentile head in all the family home movies, while shaking his middle finger at the camera woman, my poor mother. My grandfather made my dad look like Ward Cleaver.

I don't know what my father was thinking when I relayed Paul's advice to him. It must have been a kaleidoscope of events and feelings from his own life: his pride in Paul's accomplishments; the value he placed on being a West Point graduate; his own college degree earned through night school classes, thirty years after he'd finished high school; the tuition he'd have to pay if I went to Holy Cross; my face, sitting on the bleachers, watching a parade of cadets march by; my mother's disappointment—still—at her own father refusing to pay the $15/month tuition at Northeastern in 1939 and instead, forcing her to go to secretarial school.

I was surprised that afternoon in February 1976, when my father said, "Don't go anywhere. I'm calling your brother back."

I heard him on the phone. "Listen, Paul, I know what you're thinking. But they're going to let women in, and when they do, they should have good women in there."

When I got on the phone, that's what Paul told me. Might as well apply, he said, and see what happens. If you don't, he said, you'll miss this opportunity that others will be given.

And so I began the application process.

two

The Admissions Process

"West Point seeks a class composition of top scholars, leaders, athletes, soldiers, women and minorities to maintain a diversified collegiate environment and corps."

— USMA Admissions Catalog, 2008-2009

In 1975, President Ford signed the law that allowed women to attend the United States Military, Naval, Air Force, and Coast Guard Academies. I applied only to the Military Academy at West Point because I was eighteen years old and I knew *everything*.

I was afraid of heights and had no desire to be above the ground in anything except a very short tree. Besides, I didn't get out of Boston's South Shore much, and Colorado might as well have been in China. That ruled out the Air Force Academy. It was too far away from Massachusetts, no Red Sox games, no Bruins, no front page photos of Ted Kennedy's latest jowl. Since the Naval Academy meant ships and I preferred to deal with the ocean while covered with baby oil reading a book on a beach chair, I ruled out Annapolis as well. I didn't know anything about the Coast Guard Academy and had no inclination to fill that knowledge gap.

The large gray envelopes from the West Point Admissions Directorate came in the mail, through the brass opening in the front door, and landed with a thud on the worn carpet. My mother placed them on the kitchen table, separating them from the bills and Sears Roebucks ads.

"They're addressed to me," I insisted, like an adolescent brat, "Don't open them!" There were piles of applications and requirements. My mother steamed over my stubbornness. I wouldn't let her even proofread.

If you want to go to West Point, you need to follow *The Plan*. *The Plan* is simple: Through all four years of high school, get mostly As, some scattered Bs. Be involved in a variety of clubs, be a leader, a president in these extracurricular activities. Play sports, varsity only; junior varsity won't cut it; and be team captain of at least one sport, more than one is best. Visit old folks at nursing homes. Give out donuts at blood drives. Build houses for humanity. Be an Eagle Scout.

The Whole Man concept applied to the admissions process before the academy was forced to accept Whole Women as well, back when "men were men and dinosaurs roamed the plains"—an old corps saying for "Before Women." The Whole Man concept meant well-rounded; they wanted academics, leadership potential and athletics. I got worried.

I didn't follow *The Plan*. I didn't even know there was one out there. I did get Sister Agnesca's vote of confidence, and that was nice, but when I read the pamphlets and saw the statistics of the incoming classes, I wished I'd known about that *Plan*.

Academically, I thought I might make the cut. I was a nerd. I was happiest sitting at a desk overflowing with reams of hand-written notes, meticulously taken in different colored pens, with underlines, little stars or flowers in the margin noting which line is more important, which phrases are testable material. I had color-coded systems for notebooks and book covers. I think I just came out of the womb this way, though it must skip a generation as God knows my kids don't have it. Due to my nerdiness, I had the grades that West Point wanted to see on those high school transcripts. So academically, it was looking OK, but, the other two categories, leadership potential and athletics were, on a good day, weak. Very weak.

I knew I should have joined Brownies in third grade. Would it help, I wondered, if I was on the math team, oratory club, English academy, National Honor Society and school newspaper? Note "on the," as in member, participant, attendee. I wasn't even in a leadership position on the math team whose members could be counted on a mitten. Actually, I was a pretty good follower. A good hard worker who neither made waves nor rocked the boat. I just paddled away, not even checking the direction I was heading, but working hard to get there.

I saw my dream fading. Why hadn't I read about the admissions criteria earlier? I could have at least tried to do something. Or maybe not. Go through fourteen years of life as a non-assertive follower and then just, bam, run for class president? I had as much leadership ability as a spring lamb in a herd of sheep.

I was initially hopeful about athletics since I really was a tomboy growing up. My favorite cut-off shorts were turquoise with a baseball patch ironed on to the behind pocket. I stayed in the house on Saturday afternoons to watch the Red Sox on Channel 38. I kept baseball cards alphabetically arranged in a green and yellow tin recipe container my mother gave me and I knew the birthdays and hometowns of every player by heart. Still, I wait for the '67 Red Sox to be a category in "Jeopardy" so I can showcase my wealth of knowledge.

Sadly, I was a wanna-be. I couldn't throw a ball across my bedroom. Nor catch it, nor hit it, but throwing was the biggest problem. I never learned how you hold a ball, how you wind that arm up, how you follow through with your wrist. I grasped the ball awkwardly, hoisted my arm up somewhere I had no idea where, and sort of flung the ball, hoping to initiate forward motion. Neon lights flashed above me and the loud speaker announced so the world could hear, "GIRL THROWING BALL! GIRL THROWING BALL!"

It was different back then. When all the mothers were housewives, life was less officially organized. Mothers were home drinking Sanka with real half-and-half and smoking Winstons at the kitchen table when we walked in the door after school. No soccer practices, no travel softball teams, no spe-

Gail (*right*), 10, shares a joke with a friend. 1969

cial tutoring. There weren't even vans back then. The mothers sat; the kids grabbed a Devil Dog or Yodel, then darted outside to play loose games, spur of the moment, make up your own rules games.

So the games I'd learned as a kid (Hit the Bat, Flashlight Tag, Four Square,etc.) were not the organized sports that would have helped me get into West Point. I skated on the frozen pond at the swamp in the woods. After dinner on Wednesday nights, I took gymnastic lessons in a dusty room, an over-sized closet really, behind the Knights of Columbus hall. When I entered high school, if balls were required, I backed off. (Some people would say I'm still that way today.)

I found something totally ball-less to do. I became a cheerleader. I was an unlikely cheerleader. I wasn't bubbly, buxom, or cute. There wasn't an effervescent bone in my body. Though I don't often admit this: I really didn't care if the team won or lost. I was usually so cold; I just wanted it to be over, one way or the other. But, according to the gobs of information that admissions had sent, cheerleading was a sport! HA! As far as athleticism goes, I knew that cheerleaders sweated less than the harried women in the snack bar, but I wasn't going to tell. Except when we did a jump or cartwheel, which wasn't very often, we probably expended the same amount of calories as those hot chocolate makers. I earned two varsity cheerleading letters for football and three for hockey. Yes, Hockey. (In a skirt, it's *cold* in those rinks.) In the aisle between the first row of seats and the rink, there isn't even room for cartwheels. We banged on the glass.

When I filled out the application forms for West Point, and circled with my number two pencil, *five* varsity letters, I had never been challenged physically in my life. I had two serious shortfalls: leadership potential and athletics. I had backed myself into somewhat of a loser corner and now I had no choice. I *had* to do well on the two big tests West Point required its applicants to take, the SAT and the Physical Aptitude Exam (PAE), now called the Cadet Fitness Assessment or CFA, or else I'd be looking for a car pool to the closest state college.

You could live in Podunk, Montana. You could travel an hour on a bus through nowhere to arrive at the high school, which housed four counties. You could be number one in your class of sixteen students, most of whose parents are married to their cousins. Enter the SAT. West Point uses these standardized tests to make sure "Mr. Podunk," despite that 4.5 GPA, will make it through his plebe year at West Point. My SATs were slightly over six hundred in each, the same score on each test, a statement to the world that I worked equally hard in every subject but showed no innate genius in any one area.

You could earn five varsity letters. You could do a perfect cartwheel and get your crotch about an inch off the ground in a split. You could clap your hands and stamp your feet at the same time and be co-captain of the football cheerleading squad. Enter the Physical Aptitude Exam (PAE). Think of it as an SAT for the biceps and hamstrings, both of which had enjoyed a life-long nap in my body. I was not excited about taking this test.

There used to be four events in the test: the flexed arm hang, a kneeling basketball throw, a standing broad jump, and a 300-yard shuttle run. I practiced. Sharon, my best friend since second grade, walked down to the high school track after school with me, armed with a stopwatch and a basketball. She also had an apple. She ate the apple while I practiced for the test. I'm still not sure why.

If I passed this test, it would rank up there with "The Feeding of Thousands with a Loaf of Bread" miracle.

Test day was a blistery, cold January Sunday afternoon. It encapsulated the four-year West Point experience. My parents dropped me off. They were not allowed to watch. I was the only female among forty-four males. The boys stared and gawked and didn't know what to make of me. Immediately, I had a crush on a muscular, brown-haired guy with a great smile, in a blue and white gut shirt. I had a thing for gut shirts. We were paired up together on the shuttle run. I saw him only at the start and he could have showered by the time I finished. I bombed the test.

Paul's roommate's brother worked at the Pentagon in a job that was somehow involved with the integration of women at the service academies. My dad called him and told him my results. He told my father that I didn't set any Academy records and that if I did get in to West Point, I would probably survive academically, but athletically, I'd be in trouble. No longer was I hearing only votes of confidence about this great West Point idea that I had. I didn't know if I'd get in. If I did get in, no one seemed to think I could finish.

I wanted Sister Agnesca back.

✦ ✦ ✦ ✦

"The training on the athletic field which produces…the attributes of fortitude, self-control, resolution, courage, mental ability, and of course, physical development, is one completely fundamental to an efficient soldiery."

— General Douglas MacArthur

Nearly every Saturday, Josie got her mother's lime green Pinto with the fake wooden paneling down the side and drove Sharon, Kim and me to the South Shore Plaza. We would wander through Filene's and Jordan Marsh's and then wait in the line that snaked out the front door of Brigham's Ice Cream Shoppe and around the corner to the tobacco store. When we got our booth, we all would order the Brigham's Special: $1.21 for a hamburger, fries and Tab. We'd always leave the plaza to make the 4:00 pm mass before the Gospel so the mass would count. After the Gospel, the nuns told us, was too late. You'd have to go to another mass later. Going to mass was like shaving your legs. You did it without thinking because you had to.

But on the second Saturday in February, when snow crunched under your boots and the sky remained a steady somber grey, I sat on the couch under the red and white afghan my Aunt Alice had knitted, reading *Stranger in a Strange Land* for Mr. Loughmann's English class. Josie was in Vermont visiting her old Aunt Tiny; Sharon was working at the plaza shoe store; Kim was baby-sitting. Thump at the door. My mother picked the mail up off the floor. She tilted her head, which she did sometimes when she was thinking, then looked over at me. "Something from West Point," she said. It was big and gray. I jumped up. *Would they spend all that money for postage if it were a rejection?*

My mother was a hugger. My father was not. But he was emotional. I couldn't tell what he was thinking. He congratulated me, but then he paused, hesitating. Waiting. Like he had something crucial to say. I looked up at him. He picked up one of the information pamphlets that came in the grey packet and he glanced at the photo, a serious-looking cadet wearing a green helmet, beads of sweat shining over green painted cheeks, carrying a big black gun, in the woods. My father sighed. My father was not a sigher. My father was a "burst out with his thoughts" kind of guy; a "let my mother pick up the pieces later" kind of dad. This sigh meant he must have been reading parenting magazines. Finally, he put the photo of Patton, Jr. on the table, then asked me, "Honey, do you think you should start running or something?"

Poor Dad. He would always be baffled by the female psyche, and be very content to not go there. Not enough warmth in his childhood or something. He didn't know how to deal with this eighteen-year-old cheerleader. Can you blame him? What a parenting dilemma: do you encourage a child to do something that you know is really, really, really hard, something that you're confident she cannot do, something you're sure she'll fail at?

My father didn't know the answer. He didn't know what to think, what to do that February afternoon. He spent the next four years that way.

I told him sure, not to worry, I'd start running.

I spent two months buying cute T-shirts, matching socks and hair ribbons. When April hit, I jogged with Arthur, a friend who lived four doors up who wanted to make the summer basketball league team. He was 6'6" and I was 5'3"—Mutt and Jeff, jogging down Washington Street, past Richmond's Hardware and Henry's Pub, around Tremont Street, the double-decker houses and Venuti's Funeral Home, then back to the top of Robinson Avenue, three of the longest miles I'd ever seen in my life. Anyway, I was more concerned about looking cute in my matching outfits than getting in shape.

Later in life, my mother got cancer. She didn't seem to want to know the facts of her illness. I couldn't understand why. She knew: Sometimes being clueless makes it easier to go to hard places.

Four Eggheads from my high school were going to West Point. All the incoming freshmen at Archies took a diagnostic test and thirty of us, based upon the results of that test, were put in one homeroom, took advanced math and science classes together and were officially called "Eggheads." Four of us—Patty Mahoney, Jimmy McConville, Mike McGrath and me—out of a graduating class of 206 from our high school received appointments to West Point. That's a lot.

I wasn't sure what I felt about these classmates of mine joining me on my big adventure. Their company meant less glory for me! Mike was captain of the football team, one of six McGrath boys with an older brother at Norwich. He was reserved and quiet, not a conversation initiator, and since I wasn't either, we'd never said boo to each other. Jimmy was funny, almost a wise-guy, really smart, full of potential, not so full of effort. Both Jimmy and Mike were from Quincy—one town over—and I didn't know either of them well enough to decide what I thought about them at West Point. I didn't care really; I figured they'd be fine. It was me I was worried about.

Patty surprised me the most. I'd known her since half-day kindergarten at Monatiquot Elementary School. We hung out in different crowds; she was more sociable than I was, though some trees were, too. She attracted boys like I attracted pimples. She was too normal to want to go to West Point. I didn't get why she wanted to go. For some reason, it was OK for me to want to go, but not for *normal* girls.

Mr. Mahoney drove Patty and me in their Ford station wagon to visit West Point on a bright and warm April Saturday. He'd called Admissions and set up a short tour since Patty had never visited, and I really only knew how to do tailgates at Buffalo Soldier Field and football games at Michie Stadium. It was weird being at West Point not as a little sister. I was a pre-candidate, not there visiting someone else; I was there for me. I was excited to the point of nausea; I wanted to tell everyone that I was going to be a cadet next year. *Oh, please!*

We stood near a towering statue of Eisenhower and met Billy, blue eyed, handsome, blond, and kind. He was the head rabble-rouser, the West Point lingo for cheerleader and the admissions officer had arranged for him to show us around for a few hours. I'd never thought about being a cheerleader at West Point, though way back, hidden in the vanity closet of my mind, was the notion that being a college cheerleader would surpass all self-expectations of coolness. Billy wanted to introduce us to some female cadets; there were less than a hundred of them there at this time (only sixty-two would graduate three years later), all plebes in the first class of women, the Class of 1980.

We left Mr. Mahoney with the tourists and parents and Patty and I followed Billy across an open cement area and into a grey six-story building, up five flights of grey stairs that echoed with yelling and chaos. So exciting!

"They'll be getting ready for the parade," Billy told us. "This will probably not be the best time for y'all to chat." What a great smile. Patty and I melted, too enamored to appreciate the chaos around us, too stupid to think of ourselves as ever being a part of it.

Billy knocked on a brown wood door. We heard someone yell something through the door, and he opened it for us to see that a small tornado had just touched down. Billy laughed and introduced a dark-haired girl to us as Danna. He shooed us in the room and closed the door, leaving us in the room while he stayed in the hallway. White starched belts, brass cleaner, shoe polish, rifle-cleaning rods were scattered on the beds and the desks. Two other girls, one tall redhead and one short brunette, were scurrying, doing things to each other's shirts and fiddling with the buckles and belts that draped over their shoulders. There was yelling in the hallways. The minute callers, Danna told us. It's a plebe duty, she explained. "Do you guys really want to come here?" She asked, as she grabbed her rifle off the bed. Patty and I looked at each other. She laughed. "Ok, if you do, get your haircut before you come! Don't let them cut it at the barber shop!" And then, holding her rifle in front of her, up and down, like a vertical line, she apologized for being in a rush, then charged out the door.

"Nice girl," Patty said as we joined Billy again in the hallway.

"She is," he agreed. "But it hasn't been easy."

Patty and I looked at each other. We had something in common: neither one of us could refuse a challenge. Of course, Patty will take on a challenge and somehow attract boys. When I take on a challenge, my face breaks out.

After the parade, we walked with Billy into the mess hall, where a few thousand male cadets and those hundred or so female cadets were eating lunch. Patty and I both wore '70s stuff: close-fitting skirts that flared a bit below the knee, summer blouses, harachi sandals. Long straight brown hair hung halfway down our backs, killer tans, not Playboy bunny material, but not dirt ugly either. "It won't exactly be like this when y'all get here in July," Billy smiled.

"Huh?" we asked. And that's how we left our visit. In a daze, completely enamored and totally clueless.

It was probably easier that way.

✦ ✦ ✦ ✦

"Eden is that old-fashioned house we dwell in everyday, without suspecting our abode, until we drive away."

— Emily Dickinson

An interesting thing happens when you want something badly, and then boom, there it is, you've got it; it's going to happen; and then, if you allow yourself to think about it, it's not as if you don't want it anymore, but it sure doesn't look as good as it did when you wanted it so badly. This is what happened with R-Day. The closer it got, the more real it got, the more worried I got, the less enticing it looked.

I had a list of "Things to Do Before West Point." Some of the things made no sense at all: a peanut buster parfait at Dairy Queen and chocolate crème puff at Valle's Steakhouse with Josie, a lot of sleep, a killer tan. Some of the things made a lot of sense: breaking in the combat boots I had to buy, getting my long straight brown hair cut for the first time in years, like that nice girl had recommended. And then there were some things that didn't make the list because I just didn't want to think about them…. like saying good bye to family and friends.

I met Kathy before Sean. I was in seventh grade and I was not an animal lover, but a gang of us were in her backyard looking at whatever she had. They were gerbils or hamsters; I still don't know which is which. I thought they looked like big rodents—their tails were particularly ugly—so I stood back from the group. Kathy was in sixth grade and was new. Her family had just moved to Braintree from California, which was like moving into the neighborhood from Mars. I didn't know she had a brother.

Sean rode his bike up the driveway, ignoring the commotion near his sister, parked it in the garage, then walked past us, up the back steps and into the house.

"Who was that?" Pamela Smith asked. I wasn't surprised. She wore make up and shorts that rode half-way up her butt. She was keeping a cool distance from the big rats, too.

It didn't take Pamela long. She and Sean were hiding together during flashlight tag before the end of the week. I followed them around like a puppy dog. They finally broke up. I continued to follow him around, but it took him two and a half years to notice. The summer before tenth grade, he asked me out.

He was going pre-med to Stonehill, a college about twenty miles away. When I'd be walking around the woods wearing green paint on my face, he'd be drinking beer at frat parties. This concerned me.

The night before I left for West Point, they threw a party for me at Sean's house. Sharon, and Kim, who waited for me every day after kindergarten, gave me a powder blue suitcase with my initials on it, and they ate too much spiked watermelon. Sean and I left the party early. I cried a lot. He knew me better than anyone; he knew Braintree was too small for me. We agreed to write and he said he'd visit with my parents the first time we were allowed to have company mid-July, but I knew it would never be the same. If he had been the one going to West Point, we could have managed this long-distance relationship. But he wasn't the one going to West Point. It was me. And I knew I'd have to cut all emotional ties to home if I had any chance at all of surviving.

three

R-Day: July 6, 1977

My R-Day meant another family vacation. The last family vacation we took was in the Dodge Colt, all four of us, driving down I-95 to Springfield, Virginia to see Cousin Cathy graduate from high school in 1973. Family vacations were hard because we didn't have much of a family, but my mother did such a great job at faking we were the Cleavers, I almost started to believe it myself.

My father told me this story after my mother died. When she was eight years old, leaning over a cement water fountain for a drink at a park near her double-decker house in Dorchester, some kid whammed her from behind. She lost her two front teeth. Gone. This was the late twenties, depression-era time and there was no money to replace the teeth. My mother had no front teeth and no one ever knew. She learned how to smile without ever showing that gummy gap in her mouth. She didn't get those front teeth until she was engaged to my father and he bought them for her. All that time, through her teenage years, she had no front teeth and no one ever knew. This is how she lived her life: smiling without showing what was missing. Her glass was always half full.

So, with my mother at the controls, our R-Day family vacation would happen, no matter what. Garrett, my oldest brother, ten years older than me, had "gone out West" where, according to my mother, he worked on a boys' ranch. Paul, the Army aviator, was in South Korea protecting it from the spread of communist aggression. Fred, two years younger than me, sweet talked my mother into letting him stay home and I didn't blame him. The last R-Day we did wasn't much fun. Who'd want to spend another endless eight hours watching sweaty, skinny white shirts that all looked alike and listening to my mother say, *Is that her? Or is that? I think that was her. Oh, no—it wasn't.*

My mother's sister Aunt Rita and her husband, Uncle Gerard, stepped in for my missing siblings and drove with my parents and me to West Point for my R-Day. My parents had learned the tricks of being a cadet parent through Paul's experiences, so we stayed at the Hotel Thayer, the historic hotel located on West Point that looked like it stepped off a game piece from our Stratego board with its stone façade and turrets. The open, airy, lobby was loaded with coats of arms and fretting parents and other nervous candidates. Their energy fed me the breakfast I couldn't eat. I couldn't swallow my scrambled eggs. I couldn't sit still. I just wanted to get the show on the road.

Mr. Mahoney organized the four of us, Patty, Jimmy, Mike and me, for pictures in front of the hotel before we left for Gillis Field House. We had the same look that Neil Armstrong must have had when he gazed around at the other astronauts before taking off for the moon: Do we really want to go here? We loaded a shuttle bus and drove up Thayer Road, and then the bus stopped and we got off on a crowded sidewalk that overlooked the field house.

My father wanted to carry my suitcase and I wouldn't let him.

"I have it, Dad," I insisted.

"Don't be foolish," he insisted back.

I argued with him, yanking it from his hands. From where I sat in life, I was saving him from a heart attack. He was too old to carry my suitcase down the hill. He was fifty-four!

My mother shook her head and I heard her mutter to her sister, "Little Miss Tough as Nails."

I supposed she was referring to me. It was not until I became a mother of teenagers that I realized the enormity of patience my mother had. That R-day morning, I'm quite certain she had wanted to refer to me as a "Stubborn Independent Little Bitch." She may have thought "Tough as Nails" sounded more motherly. Or, more likely, she was just trying to convince herself that I was "tough as nails"; that her ninety-eight-pound daughter who had never done anything hard in her life, who had never fired a gun, who had never hiked in the woods, who had never sweated from physical exertion, was going to be OK.

I carried my powder blue suitcase down the hill, in and out of slow grandparents and dawdling candidates, and when we stepped onto the wide cement stairs that led into the field house, we'd lost the McConvilles and Mc-

Graths in the crowd, but somehow had stuck close to the ten Mahoneys.

How I envied the Mahoneys. All eight children—Patty was fourth, smack in the middle—were there for R-Day. We sat near them in the bleachers. A man wearing a uniform was talking into a microphone, how great we were, how proud our parents should be, how exciting our journey would be and then, like an all-business doctor in the delivery room, he gave us ninety seconds to say good-bye to our families before he whacked the umbilical cord.

The Mahoneys wailed. They were an emotional lot.

I got hairy nostrils and an outward lack of emotions from my father. I wasn't much of a hugger. Embarrassed, I endured the hugs of my mother, Aunt Rita,

Gail carrying her suitcase to the field house R-Day, July 6, 1977

and Uncle Gerard, all solid embracers, then my father, who was a pat-the-back hugger. My mother's face, chin to forehead, went red. She pinched her lips together and brought her hands up to her mouth, a sign of worry. Her eyes watered and filled and this was my cue to exit quickly. Everything my mother did was based upon how it would affect other people. She would explode before she cried in front of me. She knew if she cried, if she let it rip, I would have felt bad. She knew if she cried, it would have made it harder for me to leave and so she stayed strong; she smiled with no front teeth, to ease the separation for me.

I refused to cry. I picked up my powder blue suitcase and I didn't look back.

✦ ✦ ✦ ✦

R-Day is like childbirth, except it happens in reverse order and on R-Day, I didn't throw up or have back pain. Reverse order: On R-Day, the umbilical cord is sliced at the field house. The rest of the day is like a twenty-four hour labor, off-the-chart contractions, crashing into each other, no breaks, no drugs. All those Lamaze classes just don't help a bit. You think: *When is this going to be over? Why did I get myself in this mess? What was I possibly thinking?* When it's finally over, you sigh loudly, *I can't believe I*

The "Four Eggheads" from Archbishop Williams High School, Class of 1977 on R-Day: (*left to right*) Jimmy McConville, Gail O'Sullivan, Patty Mahoney and Mike McGrath

*signed up for this! How did I survive that? Never again! But what's this? They're talking about **more**? An after-birth? I thought I was done!* I'd watched Paul's experience through the delivery room window and it looked like he was handling the pains well, what a champ. Until I experienced it, I never really knew an R-Day.

I stuck close to Patty, lugging that sky blue suitcase, following the crowd of bewildered eighteen year olds across the floor of the field house and out the doors, down the stairs and onto a bus. Patty and I shared a seat on the bus. A girl with brown eyes as big as dinner plates, wavy dark brown hair and a nervous half-smile sat behind us. I wondered about the girls. I wondered what they'd be like. I wondered if they'd be normal. She said her name was Liz and she was from New York City. She sounded tougher than she was; she admitted being scared to death. But she laughed easily and she looked normal! What *normal* girl would want to go to a place like this? Was I *normal*?

Our bus crept up the hill from the river to Arvin Gymnasium. Before we got comfortable, the ride was over. I should have enjoyed the sights more. Our welcoming committee stood in front of the wooden doors to the gym.

Upper-class cadets, jittery with impatience, hands on their waists, red cheeked, and tight lipped. Their eyes were glaring so hard, it *had* to hurt. *This is not a good sign*, I thought. I'd seen the uniform before, but they sure didn't look this mean when they were drinking beer and eating roast beef subs behind the white Dodge Colt after football games. And didn't they use to be handsome? It suddenly became very weird. We weren't in Kansas, anymore, Toto.

They shuffled us off the bus and like a pack of wild dogs, began to bark at us, barked to keep our eyes straight ahead, barked to not talk to anyone, barked to do a zillion things by a zillion different people. Upper-class cadets, all wearing white starched shirts and grey pants, white hats and shiny black shoes, some with fancy blood-red sashes hanging from their waist, all looking ceremoniously grave, were everywhere. It *could* have been scary, but after twelve years of nuns, I was used to generally unhappy people who wore uniforms and yelled a lot. Instead, I thought *what organization*! I thought how much my father would have loved this. He loved the mess hall. It was incredible; he marveled out loud, that they could feed four thousand cadets in one sitting in twenty minutes. It was too bad he couldn't see this gym! Tables scattered across the basketball court, hundreds of us lined up one behind the other, standing at attention, eyes straight ahead, not talking, not moving, a minimal wait, then a bark and a point and we filed to the next table. We got shots. We stepped on scales. I held my breath, frightened they would send me home. I breathed in and didn't exhale. A bald man in a gray shirt wrote "99" down on the paper. He didn't skip a beat. He pointed me to the next table and I exhaled. No one seemed to care about my weight after all.

We filled out forms. We did pull-ups. Well, most of us did. I was ashamed and embarrassed when they put a big goose egg on my paper. I wanted to explain, to apologize, "I'm sorry. I wish I could! But I can't!" They wouldn't let me say anything. All I could do was look ashamed and embarrassed, staring straight ahead at attention.

They hustled us out of the gym. They whipped us, really, without a whip, this way and that, through a tunnel into an open, dusty room with long tables and short tailors and gray wool. They issued us gray pants, the exact same ones that Frank our mailman wore. We zipped around in white undershirts, mailman pants and black nun shoes, with a wad of papers pinned to our pants so we'd know what station we had to go to next. This was not your regular college freshman orientation day. The nun shoes alone assured that.

It was like musical chairs outside, in the area between the grey barracks buildings, to the beat of a single drum and with no prizes. We were in groups of eight or so, then, one or two of us were whisked away to be fitted for shoes (unusually high arches or wide feet) or military issue glasses (hideous huge black frames that later we'd call BCDs (Birth Control Devices). If you looked *anywhere*, someone would see you and yell at you. *Eyes straight ahead, new cadet! Quit your gazing around, new cadet!* We could only look straight ahead and that meant not seeing who was coming, who was going. We could just feel the shift in the background, like at the dentist, in that chair, knowing there are people behind you, but you're stuck still and uncomfortable, with those white fingered gloves up your mouth.

We were rarely alone. We were surrounded by upperclassmen, stern, angry, really-need-to-lighten-up upperclassmen. Their job was to teach us everything we needed to know and more. We learned how to march, left foot hitting the ground to the beat of the drum. Forward march, right turn march, mark time march, halt. Marching became our preferred mode of transportation. If there were more than one of us in a group, we marched. If sent out on a solo mission—"New Cadet O'Sullivan, take your duffel bag to your room. Use the latrine. Drink water. Then fall in back here ASAP!"—then we "pinged", which meant walking 180 steps per minute at attention. *Who timed these steps?* They also spouted something about our arms, "Nine to the front, six to the rear", but I missed the translation and wasn't going to ask, so didn't learn until months later that we were supposed to swing our arms nine inches to the front and six inches to the rear. *Who measured?*

We learned how to salute. We learned how to report to the Man in the Red Sash. He was obviously the Grand Pooh-bah, a very big deal. There were lines of new cadets, most in their white T-shirts and gray pants, though some, not yet issued their pants, presidents of their senior class, captains of their football teams, now looking like Mr. Ialenti working in his tomato garden with gym shorts and knee high black socks with black leather shoes. We waited in line to see one of the four cadets who stood in their starched white shirt against the barracks wall, like someone had stuck broomsticks up their butts. These four cadets wore red sashes and obviously thought that they were more important than they really were. A lanky, scar-faced, pimply cadet taught me and six of my new best friends how to salute, taught us what to say, taught us how to stop before the white line, not on it, not over it, just millimeters before it. How could we see the white line if we couldn't look down? It was a mystery. I marched to the back of the line to report to the Man in the Red Sash, for the first time.

I should have used more deodorant. Sweat dripped down every body part, slowly, in plops, and I felt dirty and smelly and miserable. My new grey pants itched. My new black socks stuck to my toes, smooshing them together. I was on deck, next up. I went over the litany in my head: *Sir, New Cadet O'Sullivan reports to the man in the red sash for the first time as ordered.* You had to do *every* little thing right! The kid in front of me flustered. His back muscles told the story. They were all I could see as I stared straight ahead, like a good new cadet, and that meant staring at his wet T-shirt where I could watch his muscles go from twitch to shudder to defeat. The upper-class cadet with the red sash yelled DO I LOOK LIKE A RED SASH? Geez, do they have to bark everything, I thought. The back muscles drooped and then the new cadet in front of me turned, marching to the back of the line again.

I was up. I popped my hand up and out came the cadet's hand. He stopped me mid-salute. So much for my memorized litany; I couldn't even get past the salute. Something about my fingers and my wrist, the Man in the Red Sash was saying. "New Cadet, may I touch you?" *Like I have a choice? Can I really tell Mr. Cheerful, no, sorry, keep your paws to yourself!?* He adjusted my salute gingerly, like I had cooties. Then, loudly, so most of the Northern Hemisphere could hear, he announced: **Go to the back of the line! Try again, New Cadet!** Back in line, I'm practicing in my head, over and over, again and again drilling that sentence into my thick skull. After four trips to the back of the line, my salute finally won approval though I had no clue what I did differently, and I got the words right, and the Man in the Red Sash told me to report upstairs to the third floor, Seventh Company, Hellfire and Brimstone. Whatever that meant.

We walked against the walls, right up next to them, just inches from them, and we squared our corners, which meant that if we wanted to go a different direction, we had to do a fancy foot movement, a right turn or a left turn. Gone were the days of just turning your body like a normal person. When we went up or down stairs, our forearms were held up, near our chest, for crying out loud, and parallel to the ground. I thought we must look like twits. I was left in my room for a few minutes alone. I was supposed to find the latrine and drink water, that's what one of them had told me to do, but I didn't want to go back out in that hall where all those pests in the white shirts were. I exhaled and breathed and looked out the window at the chaos below in the area. Then I turned and I looked around the room, my new home, for the first time. Petro was on the paper nametag on the other bed. My roommate: Petro. It didn't sound Irish. I stared at the two plain wooden desks, two grey steel framed beds, two bare wardrobes. Did it look this much like a prison when I visited?

It may have been a female thing, but more than almost anything else, I worried about meeting my roommate. I wondered, after a few hours, if they planned it so we'd never be in the room at the same time. I couldn't hang around to wait for her. I had to go back out there. I didn't want to, but I opened the door and sprint-walked across the hall to walk down the hall against the wall, found the door marked WOMENS LATRINE, no easy task with your head straight ahead—*this place was going to give my eyeballs a workout*—I darted in, drank some water from the fountain, and then dragged myself back outside to find the man who had told me to go to the latrine and drink water. No roommate along the way. Later, when I dropped off my duffel bag in the room, hers wasn't there yet. Even more later, when another angry man in white told me to go to the latrine again and drink water, her duffel bag was there, but she was not. Finally, even later, years after I'd picked at scrambled eggs with my parents at the Hotel Thayer restaurant; I landed in the room with my roommate for the same two- minute splash of time. Her name was Janet. She was tanned and blond, pretty, from Florida, and had a funny accent. I knew I'd like her and I was so relieved. The only good thing that had happened all day: my roommate looked nice.

Back down in the area between the barracks buildings with a thousand of my new best friends, I remembered Paul's advice on the phone, "Play it low-profile." The female thing never entered my mind. Every brain cell was concentrating on doing every little thing right; I had no brain cells left to think about being a female, to think about being different, to being un-welcome. It didn't look to me like *any* of us were being greeted with warm and fuzzy hugs.

I didn't think that I was getting yelled at more than anyone else, though Miss Nosey Britches had a hard time not gazing around. I thought I saw, in the crowd of people standing behind the chain keeping them out of the barracks area, two people who looked just like my parents, but I got nabbed trying to discreetly rotate my eyes without moving my head. "Cut the gazing around, New Cadet!" These guys don't miss a trick, I thought. When my mother sent the pictures of me reporting to the man with the red sash, I realized that couple *was* my parents. I thought I saw Jimmy Mac, from high school, out of the corner of my eye. It would have been nice, a bit comforting, to see someone familiar in this chaos, but it was hard to see much of anything when you're looking straight into the belt buckle of a big guy who seemed to be angry about something.

The upperclassmen didn't just yell at me. They yelled at everyone. And to be literal, true yelling was in fact rare. They "corrected" everyone. Their "corrections" weren't always in the nicest tone of voice, but they didn't raise their voice to the decibel level that Mrs. Monti used calling in the thirteen Montis for dinner. (No kidding. There were thirteen of them. Mrs. Monti had potent vocal cords.) Usually, the yelling was at the same level as Bloody, whose real name was Sister Catherine Pickens, my high school French teacher who put at least one student in tears daily. Not screaming, just nasty and mean.

New cadets in the Class of 1981 reporting to the "Man in the Red Sash"

They were all over one new cadet, like flies to honey. He was built like a fire hydrant, even shorter than I was, but with shoulders quadruple mine in width. Though white hats towered over him from every direction, he forged invisible armor around his stocky frame, deflecting all attention with a smirk. There was something about his demeanor. I'll admit it. I was glad, relieved, that he was the one getting all the attention from the upperclassmen. One thing I learned in Catholic grade school was that when a nun picks on Joey Shaughnessy, it decreases the time she has to pick on you.

My watch said 4:30 p.m., though the upperclassmen kept calling it 1630. They shouted, all at the same time, something about a shower, a proper uniform, and a formation for the parade. I thought, in the midst of the commotion, this is why they made us cut our hair, no time to blow dry, no time to go to the bathroom, no time to think. Janet and I were back in our room, only the second time that the two of us had been together all day. We looked at each other like we had just found out our mothers were axe murderers. *No way can this be happening!* We shook our heads, feeling the panic that was setting in, and told each other there was no way we could be ready, showered and dressed in that white shirt, mailman pants, white cap, and black shoes in twenty minutes. *Were they nuts?*

We raced down the hall, walking against the wall, eyes straight ahead, really fast. I followed Janet and stayed right behind her. We turned the corner to go into the bathroom. Someone yelled, "New Cadets, Halt!"

Us? We stepped back out into the hall. *We don't have time to halt!* "Go back down MY hall and try it again! Square MY corner before you go into that latrine!" *Gawd, is he serious? Does he realize we are in a time crunch here?* We race back down the hall, against the wall, eyes straight ahead, breathing so fast it hurts, to our room, open the door, step in, step out, close the door, back across the hallway, against the wall. We exaggerate our squaring the corner, then duck in the latrine.

The latrines, the West Point word for bathroom, were safe zones, for us females in that second class. There were no upper-class women around. The upperclassmen who ran Beast Barracks were all seniors, known as "firsties," with a handful of juniors, called cows. The only upper-class women were sophomores, the yearlings, who were doing their summer training eight miles away from West Point at Camp Buckner. In the latrines, we were safe to whisper, whine and cry. I never thought a bathroom would give me such relief.

There were six stalls and four sinks on one side of the latrine, and grey metal lockers and a shower room on the other side. I found a locker that had an O'SULLIVAN name tag over it, tore off my sticky clothes, covered myself with the white bath towel, and then raced over to the shower room. I stopped short in the doorway and stared. Six shower heads splattered water all over the floor and the three girls standing there showering, naked as jay-birds.

I'd never seen another girl naked. And I really didn't want to. I'd never taken a shower with someone else. This was also on my list of *Things I Didn't Want To Do*. A big black iron rack on wheels with a few shower curtains hung haphazardly over it, stood against one wall, an attempt by the administration to provide privacy for those of us who wanted it. I wanted it. Holding the towel over my small personal parts with one hand (reality check here: flat women can't tie a towel around themselves like you see on TV—they have to hold the towel to keep it up), I grabbed the iron rack with the other hand and tried to move it toward the open shower head. It didn't budge. One of the girls who was showering had seen my chin drop to my knees when I rounded the corner. She shook her head, then said, in an odd mid-Western twang I'd only heard before on "Bonanza," "Just forgit it. You don't have time and we're not going to look at you!"

I forced a smile and let go of the rack, hung my towel over the top of it, found a free shower head, then watched my modesty wash down the drain.

New cadets in the Class of 1981 marching in the oath ceremony on the Plain.
July 1977

✤ ✤ ✤ ✤

"I, Gail O'Sullivan, do solemnly swear that I will
support the Constitution of the United States, and bear
true allegiance to the National Government; that I will maintain
and defend the sovereignty of the United States, paramount to
any and all allegiance, sovereignty, or fealty I may owe to any State
or country whatsoever: and that I will at all times obey the legal
orders of my superior officers, and the Uniform Code of Military Justice."

— Excerpt from the West Point Oath

Who knew what we were saying? We gave this Oath the same mindless
pinging that we'd given everything else that day. Over 1,200 bald-headed and
bewildered new cadets stood at attention, thumbs behind the seams of our
damp grey trousers, smeared with sweat, on the plain, the grassy parade
grounds. Even if I'd thought about what I was saying (instead of wondering if
my parents could pick me out from wherever they were sitting in the bleachers), I wouldn't have "gotten" it. I was too young, too self-absorbed, too invin-
cible. The seeds are only sown on R-Day. The cultivation takes years.

We heard the stories of the new cadets who had just up and left. Already! Forget this, they'd said, and walked away from it all, to find their parents and a ride back home. I wondered how they'd found the time during the day to even think about quitting. I wondered how they could do it. I could never. Not because I wanted to be an Army officer, not because I had a duty concept, not because the words Duty, Honor, Country meant squat to me. Really, I stayed only because I would have been too embarrassed and humiliated to quit. Everyone in Braintree knew I was at West Point. At Henry's Pub, the regulars, the WWII vets who grumbled about Guadalcanal, the Sox, and the leaky roof at the old American Legion building, had wagers on how long I'd last. I had to prove them wrong.

It turns out that cadets go to and stay at West Point for varied reasons. I'd soon meet other cadets who were there to prove something, too. The problem is that sometimes when you're doing something to prove something, you might just wake up one morning and decide you're done proving; you don't have to do it anymore. The ideal situation is you do something because you really want to do it. This way, you're more apt to wake up and keep doing it. An interesting psychological phenomenon though has been found to occur in the cadets who are trying to prove something. Whether they realize it or not, they're subconsciously buying stock in the business and at some point, they've invested so much into it; they realize that they really do want it.

On R-Day, I hadn't bought any stock. I only stayed because I'd be too embarrassed to leave.

After the Oath Ceremony on the plain, the upperclassmen marched us straight into the mess hall. We didn't know that. They could have marched us to Idaho and we would have just kept marching. We were drained empty, drenched in sweat, hungry, thirsty, and deserted. Our parents, families, girlfriends and boyfriends were getting in their cars and driving away, driving back home, and we wouldn't be home again until Christmas. We were stuck in this hot, grey, mean place, and as we pinged into the mess hall, with our eyes straight ahead, with our forearms parallel to the ground, we felt worse than we looked.

During Beast Barracks, our table commandant was our squad leader, the upperclassman responsible for the eleven new cadets in 2nd Squad, 3rd Platoon, 7th Company, "Hellfire and Brimstone, Sir." Our God, Cadet O'Dowd. He was huge. He looked like a blond Hun, over six feet tall with 220 pounds of muscle, bulging from his fatigue shirt sleeve. His cheeks were either sunburned or just bright red which made everything he said in a strong New

Jersey accent, sound a bit harsher than he meant it to sound. I was petrified of him.

He was a teddy bear. But, story of my life, it took me weeks to figure this out and by the time I did, he'd left us for his summer leave. That first night at dinner, Cadet O'Dowd spouted instructions. They just kept coming and each one seemed dumber than the one before it. He seriously laid out the guidelines on how to eat (or not eat) as a plebe at West Point: Keep your eyes fixed on the USMA crest on your plate. Pick up your knife and fork. Cut a bite-size—*Way smaller than that, New Cadet!*—piece of meat. Spear the piece you cut (there should be room on the fork for about three more regular sized pieces). Put the knife and fork down. Put your hands on your lap. Keep your eyes on the crest on your plate. Chew the meat. Put the piece of meat (unidentifiable taste, somewhere between ground beef and beef jerky) in your mouth. Swallow. Repeat the process and you'd better still be staring at the U.S.M.A. crest on your plate. I didn't have a ravenous appetite, so this strange dining ritual didn't bother me. But for guys who had spent the past twelve years grabbing everything within reach at the family dining table and wolfing it down, it was torture.

Meal time wasn't about eating. During Beast Barracks, there were ten seats at a table, one for the big wig, the upperclassman serving as table commandant, and the other nine for the peons, the new cadets. The three new cadets at the end of the table opposite the table commandant had "Table Duties." This place was going to be big on duties, I could tell already. Cadet O'Dowd explained the table duties that first night at dinner and did he really think we were going to remember all this stuff?

The Beverage Corporal sat in the chair that was directly across from the table commandant and, after everyone had been seated (we knew when to do this because a booming voice said over a microphone from somewhere in the Mess Hall heavens, "TAKE SEATS"), the Beverage Corporal, captain of his high school lacrosse team or president of her senior class, sitting erect in the chair, held up the pitcher, stared straight ahead, and announced, "Sir, the beverage for this meal is fruit punch. Would anyone not care for fruit punch, Sir?"

Probably taken from some ancient mute tradition, "Sticking one's paw out" is the West Point way to get your point across without having to actually talk. If you did not want fruit punch, you stuck your paw out, by raising your forearm, parallel to the table, with the fist closed and thumb up. The Beverage Corporal poured the appropriate number of glasses, sitting at attention, eyes straight ahead when not focused on the glasses or fruit punch.

The new cadet stuck in the seat to the right of the Beverage Corporal ably assisted him, by using a spoon to place ice cubes in the empty glasses. We learned in the next few days, that certain upperclassmen had ice requirements (one cube when there is fruit punch, two cubes for iced tea, no cubes if the weather outside is below sixty degrees, etc.). These upperclassmen were perhaps forgotten middle children or the victim of bullying in their younger years.

The Gunner, who sat in the seat on the other side of the Beverage Corporal, was the dessert cutter. Holding the dessert up with his right hand, he announced, "Sir, the dessert for this meal is Martha Washington Sheet Cake. Would anyone not care for Martha Washington sheet cake at this time?" Then he quietly hoped that an even number of people, preferably eight, wanted dessert. If only one person didn't want dessert, the gunner, if dessert was lower on his priority list than getting yelled at, might even opt to forego his own serving. Nine pieces, especially in a non-frozen cake like Martha Washington sheet cake, where cherries and vanilla pudding tumble out of the cakey part with every slice of the knife, can make a real mess. And "raping Mrs. Washington" or "massacring Mrs. Washington" was not good. (*Who said you can call her Martha, New Cadet? Did she recognize you?* Recognition was when the upperclassmen called plebes by their first name; this didn't happen until the Graduation parade in June, light years away.) Cadet O'Dowd recommended we create templates, on cardboard with a protractor, sized to fit inside the rim of our gray mailman hat. The templates would show us how to cut between three and ten pieces of cake.

I didn't make a template. I was a rule-follower and a people pleaser. Not making a template was my only act of rebellion. By winging that cake and cutting seven messy pieces, I was saying, albeit in but a whisper, "Yell at me for not cutting these pieces evenly. It just doesn't matter."

Our Beast squad gathered for the first time in a "casual" setting after dinner on R-Day in one of the barracks rooms. What a bunch. Janet grew up in Cocoa Beach, Florida, swimming, playing softball and acing through academics. She had everything that Admissions Catalog talked about.

We were the only girls in our squad. The boys were a mixed lot. Dave, Bill and Jeff were cut from the same mold, athletes and funny, just regular guys. Mark was a prepster, a graduate of USMAPS, and that made him the squad expert on anything military, shining shoes, marching, making the bed the military way. Dan was curly-haired, lanky and looked sort of stoned, from California. The most flustered by far was John. Poor John had been blessed with a family name that would pour unwarranted attention over him like hot lava. They called us, the members of the Class of 1981, by our last names. I was New Cadet O'Sullivan, a name I was proud of; content it reflected my Irish tenacity. John was New Cadet Dick.

I didn't get it. All day, people were big on the word "Dick" and I didn't know what the big deal was. Cadet O'Dowd had talked about going "Big Dick" on dessert and one of the other squad leaders had yelled at a new cadet in his squad for "Dicking on his classmates." What was this Dick deal?

I was eighteen years old and honestly had no idea that a Dick was anything other than a nickname for Richard. My mother didn't even let us say "poop," never mind "penis." So I had no idea what the huge Dick deal was. I soon realized that the male population relates everything to the anatomy. Poor John Dick must have felt humiliation beyond words as he entered this institution where the pronunciation of his last name brought smirks to the faces of thousands.

We sat and stood, on the twin beds and in the desk chairs, up against the dresser, in Bill and Dan's room and introduced ourselves to each other. Cadet O'Dowd listened, nodded his big head, smiled occasionally. Immediately, I confused him. He'd asked us what we were famous for in high school—a West Point expression. *What were you famous for in high school, New Cadet?* The implication clearly was *Enjoy the memories, because now you're not famous for squat!* I was stumped. I wasn't particularly famous for much of anything.

"Um, um,"

"Come on. O'Sullivan, you had to have done something in high school. Were you an athlete?" Even the way he asked, looking at my scrawny tanned arms, he had to have been wondering how I landed in this place. Janet had said she'd played softball and volleyball. How could I say that in 8th grade, I'd tried out for the summer parks recreation softball team but couldn't reach first base from anywhere but second so opted to join the pot-holder makers at the playground instead?

"Um, Sir, I was a cheerleader."

It just didn't feel West Point-like, tough enough, confessing to my squad and squad leader that I was famous for clapping and painting posters that said "Daze the Knights!!!" for the cafeteria. Cadet O'Dowd just shook his head, then charged into showing us how to make our rooms look like cadet rooms. Everything in its proper place, according to the blue book, the Cadet Bible of Regulations, which told us where everything's proper place was. No water stains on the water glass. Just don't use it, he recommended. Isn't that dumb, I thought. How to hang our uniforms in the closet. How to put our shoes in the wardrobe. How to fold our clothes and put them in the proper place in the drawer. He put on a serious face as he pulled open the top drawer of the dresser and looked over at Janet and me. With that Jersey accent, he said, "I dunno how to do your underwear. There's a picture in the blue book that shows you."

Back in our room, my first night ever away from home, except for occasional pajama parties at Josie's and a weekend a summer at Sharon's family cottage down the Cape, I folded my bras according to the blue book and rolled my thin black socks, the same ones my father wore with plaid shorts while he pushed the push-mower on our front lawn back home. I knew how lucky I was to have Janet as a roommate. This could be miserable, I thought, if I'd gotten a twit for a roommate. (That day would come.) Janet was as unsure as I was about this place.

We talked as we put our things away. Allowed one knick-knack, we'd both made collages, pictures cut this way and that and then placed in a single frame, a jigsaw puzzle of our previous life. We shared the stories behind the pictures, our families, friends, boyfriends. We'd both been in our high school homecoming courts. I looked at us now, in our black PT shorts and white T-shirt uniform tops, white ankle socks and sneakers, short hair matted to our heads with sweat, everything marked with our last name, referring to the blue book of regulations and I thought of a book that I'd had to read in middle school. *That was Then, This is Now.*

It was almost taps, 11:00 p.m. or as we were learning, 2300 hours, when Cinderella had to be dressed in her issued gray pajamas, a night shirt that was too see-through and very hideous. All lights had to be out and we had to be in bed.

Knock, Knock. This place even had a right way to knock!

And a right way to answer the knock. "Come in, Sir." Or "Dressing, Sir."

Janet and I looked at each other. We had clothes on. She responded, "Come in, Sir."

The door opened and an upperclassman came in. I'd seen him around. He'd yelled at me for not coming up the stairs fast enough after dinner. *Come on*, I wanted to say, but couldn't, *Give me a break! I'm tired!*

He wore the white over grey uniform and his name plate said Richards. He made sure the door stayed open by putting the small wastepaper basket in it; then he told us, too seriously, that he was our platoon leader. He explained that he was the next highest ranking cadet over our squad leader and there were four squads in his platoon, four platoons in 7th Company. He asked if we were having any problems putting our things away. *Like we were going to spill our guts and tell him our problems?* He checked our closets to make sure our uniforms were being hung properly, according to that blue book; he pulled open the drawer under our wardrobe; he looked in the medicine cabinets over the sink.

The Admissions office had sent a list of items that would help make our stay more enjoyable, stuff we were supposed to have with us when we got there. One of the toilet articles on that list was Vaseline and my mom, the bargain hunter, always on the look out for a good deal, bought me a huge vat of the stuff. Mom was always buying fifteen pounds of animal crackers, bulk shopping at discount prices, so I thought nothing of having a jar of Vaseline the size of a small pet on the bottom self of my medicine cabinet. Cadet Richards did. He held it up and laughed, an odd laugh, then said, "Come on, girls. Do you think you'll miss your boyfriends this much?" He shook his head, still laughing at his own joke; then he walked out of the room.

I didn't get it. Neither did Janet. We agreed it didn't sound good. I told Janet I thought it was "fresh", which is what my mother always called anything that was even remotely crude sounding. I didn't like him laughing at us. That was just mean. Janet and I left it hanging, the first of many *Now what do we dos?*

Knock, Knock. Enter, Sir. Cadet Richards again.

Now what's going on, I wondered. He told us to stand at ease. He looked at us with a strange expression on his face. "I'm sorry. What I just did in here was totally unprofessional and unacceptable. There is no excuse for it at all. I can only tell you that I have never been in a leadership position with female cadets under me. It's all very new to me. It won't happen again."

We didn't respond. We stood awkwardly at attention, unsure if we were supposed to respond. Janet kind of nodded. I just stood with my eyes wide and mouth open. He left the room and once again Janet and I looked at each other and shrugged. It didn't take a doctorate in leadership to figure out early on that the new cadets were the guinea pigs in the upperclassmen's leadership laboratory. That first night, I realized that these guys were going to make lots of mistakes in that lab. If they all came around like Richards did, it wouldn't be that bad, I thought.

Oh, how naïve I was.

The music played over the loud speaker. Taps. I'd heard it on TV before. Lights were switched off as the notes played. Janet and I lay on top of our beds. It was July in New York and we didn't need the covers; but, more important, we didn't want to mess the beds up and have to make them up in the morning the way Cadet O'Dowd had taught us. The room was dark, except for the glimmer of light from under the door crack and the shimmers that reflected in through the open windows.

I didn't know if we were supposed to talk. I waited to see if Janet would say anything. She did. "I'm going to miss my parents," she said softly.

"Me, too," I said.

There was scuffling in the hallway, the upperclassmen making sure we were all in bed, lights out. Lying on my back, my hands over my chest, like I was laid up at Venuti's Funeral Home; I could smell my own sweat and it wasn't pretty.

I had to ask Janet. "Did you see there are no screens on the windows here? I've never been in a room where the windows are wide open and there are no screens. Don't you think all sorts of bugs will get in here?"

It never dawned on me to worry about the lack of locks on the doors. We were in a barracks filled with men we didn't know, but I went to bed that first night at West Point, missing my parents and wondering how many bugs would greet me in the morning.

four

Beast Barracks

I'd never put my finger in a live socket before, but the shock of Beast Barracks is probably similar. Picture the cartoon character with the sticks of hair jutting out in all directions, frozen limbs a foot off the ground, bulging eyes, mouth wide open, pure terror on the face. That was me in Beast.

Beast Barracks is the Army's Basic Training, West Point style. In seven weeks, West Point takes a teenage civilian and creates a soldier-cadet. New cadets learn how to be a soldier: fire weapons, low-crawl, rappel, road march. But, they also learn how to be a cadet: fold underwear, memorize trivia, live by the honor code. All during Beast Barracks, during this indoctrination period, sleeping little, stressing much, you're referred to as "New," a leper-like adjective that your mother has to write on the address of the letters she sends you or the upperclassmen will have a small seizure. After completion of the seven weeks of training, new cadets become real cadets, not "New" any longer, and are officially accepted into the Corps of Cadets during a special parade, the Acceptance Day parade. On the day after R-Day, the Acceptance Day parade seems as far away as applying for your senior citizen discount at Shoney's.

On that first morning after R-Day, organized chaos began.

We learned how to drill. We learned how to wear our uniforms. We learned that the uniforms were not intended to be worn in 80-degree weather with 95% humidity. We learned how to properly tuck our shirts inside the pants, folding the wings like right angles, and calling them "dress

39

offs." How to shine shoes. How to shine anything that was within reach. We learned how to salute. Anything except non-commissioned officers, called NCOs, who looked the same as officers to me but liked to say, rather testily, "I work for a living" after you saluted them. NCOs weren't the only people I saluted unnecessarily that summer; the telephone repairman, who also worked for a living, but didn't feel the need to tell me that, just smiled, like it had happened to him before.

We learned our four responses.

"Yes, Sir."

"No, Sir."

"No excuse, Sir."

"Sir, I do not understand."

My all-time favorite became "No Excuse, Sir."

Really, what could they say? I wished we'd had it in grammar school. That would have shut Sister Augzentius up.

"You're right, O'Sullivan. No excuse. You're a sorry new cadet, O'Sullivan."

OK, I'm a disgrace. I'll get over it if you do. End of discussion. You had to love it.

It was nun deja-vu. Fourth classmen never initiated a conversation with an upperclassman, just like it was back in Saint Francis of Assisi with old school nuns. Fourth classmen were only allowed to respond if an upperclassman spoke to us, and our response had to be one of our four answers. We spoke freely to each other, our classmates, only in the safety of our rooms, and if there were mixed sexes in the room, the trash can had to be placed in the door to keep it open. Like I wanted to jump into bed with one of these guys in my squad?

We had to memorize "knowledge" from Bugle Notes, a handy little hard covered book full of fascinating facts: the history of West Point, academics, leadership, summer tactical training, activities, and athletics. At the back of the book was the section in ancient hieroglyphics, General Military Information, pictures of ranks, insignias, and medals which I'd never heard of or seen in my life.

How many lights in Cullum Hall?

"Two hundred forty lights, Sir."

How many names on Battle Monument?

"Two thousand two hundred and thirty names, Sir."

And my all time personal favorite. I keep waiting for someone to ask me in casual conversation. How's the cow?

"Sir, she walks, she talks, she's full of chalk, the lacteal fluid extracted from the female of the bovine species is highly prolific to the nth degree."

The ability to memorize became critical to survival. Nuns to the rescue again; all those years of them drilling facts into my head, rarely asking me to think! I memorized "Sir, the company commander is Cadet Walker." *He really looks like Robert Redford.* "Sir, the regimental commander is Cadet Hoffman." *And I hope I never get to meet him.* "Sir, the commander of Cadet Basic Training is Colonel Arvid E. West, Jr." *I've never heard the name Arvid in my life!*

Each week, we got a list of knowledge requirements and as we "passed it off", which meant while we stood at attention against the wall in the hallway, our squad leader listened to us tell him the names of the Army mules and he "checked us off." I'm not sure what would have happened if we didn't get "checked off." Would they make us do Beast again the next summer if we didn't know what the four statues in the Mess Hall represented? As we learned more and more knowledge, we passed it off at formations, since we spent most of the day standing in them anyway. We formed up to go to physical training, breakfast, classes, lunch, military drill, dinner, and the bathroom. Actually, we didn't form up to go to the bathroom. We didn't go. There wasn't time.

I arrived at West Point with some bowel issues. I was never the regular child my parents hoped for. Bowel movements were critical in my family. (My father's mood was directly proportional to his regularity.) Since I was not regular, each morning before school, I faced a bowl of hot prunes, until my mother, way ahead of her time—this was the 70s—found pure bran, in ground up form, the consistency of saw dust, in the new health food store at the South Shore Plaza. I didn't have to eat those slimy prunes anymore. I gulped down the saw dust by the tablespoon with water and met the family requirement of regularity.

My mother had visions of me not going to the bathroom for four years and truth be told, I wasn't very excited about spending my college years in a constipated state. So I packed the bag of oat bran and kept it in the bottom drawer beneath my wardrobe where we were allowed to keep *miscellaneous* items. That saw dust was as essential as toothpaste and soap.

The first time our squad leader inspected our room, he picked up the clear cellophane bag, stared at it, glanced at me, then back to the label on the bag. He turned to look directly at me. I stood at attention, waiting. I couldn't imagine getting in trouble for having oat bran in my miscellaneous drawer. It's not as if it were a Snickers bar or a Budweiser.

"O'Sullivan?" His voice was gruff and expectant. Without having to verbalize any further, between the Jersey accent and the facial expression, he said, *What the hell is this and why is it in your drawer?*

"Sir, may I make a statement?" I was good.

"Yeah, O'Sullivan. I'm dying to hear it." He had relaxed his shoulders and put his huge hands on his hips, leaning over me, not sure yet whether he should be angry.

I couldn't bring myself to make eye contact. I looked down at my shiny black shoes. This was embarrassing. Even though Janet knew about my regularity issues, my voice came out hushed.

"Sir," I began, "If I don't gulp that down with water, I won't go to the bathroom."

Cadet O'Dowd, in a practice that would become too common, shook his head in disbelief and walked out of the room. Amazingly, he didn't crack up laughing in front of me. From then on, he referred to my oat bran as "O'Sullivan's Kitty Litter."

Drill was a big deal, which makes sense if you think about the place being called a military academy, which, of course, I didn't. We spent hours on the plain, the open grassy area in front of the barracks which provided a beautiful view of the campus had we been allowed the opportunity to gaze around and enjoy it. There were certain constants about drill. It was always hot. It always smelled like cut grass that was stuffed in a wet blanket. Sweat always poured from various points on our body, soaking the white, crewneck t-shirts that we wore under our fatigue shirts. I traded the bronzed skin I had worked so hard to get, baby oil and iodine, smeared all over what wasn't covered by my two-piece, for what the upperclassmen called a "farmer's tan", coloring only on the part of the arm below the rolled up fatigue shirt. It was the beginning of the end in the Looks Department.

Drill was a piece of cake until we added the weapons. We each had an M-14A1 weapon, which looked like a big wooden gun. Unfortunately, it didn't just stay in the handsome wooden rack next to the closet in our rooms. We had to learn how to march with it, salute with it, "order arms" with it and "inspect arms" with it. It weighed more than my beach bag had weighed and I was a ninety seven pound wimp, a feeble twig with no hint of a bicep or tricep or delt. My bony, toothpick arms trembled each night as muscles that had never been woken were jolted into serious action.

I couldn't do "Inspection Arms." Standing at attention, "Inspection Arms" required you to push the bolt of the M-14 back, using the bottom part of the right hand, under the pinky finger and along the palm, while firmly holding the rifle in place at an angle across the body, with the left hand. It really bothered me, not being able to do this. It was frustrating and embarrassing and made me want to crawl into a hole. Should I even be at West Point if I couldn't do the tasks it demanded? I felt like I wasn't earning my place because I couldn't pull that bolt back. I hated Inspection Arms.

I approached everything that summer afraid. I was afraid I wouldn't be able to do it. Afraid I wouldn't earn my place in the Corps. Since those pull-ups on R-Day, "Inspection Arms" was the first thing I couldn't do. It was so important to me to be able to carry my own weight, to keep up. I had to prove that I could do this. It was what I was there for.

Guess what happens when someone who is a bit obsessive and compulsive and who wants to prove she can do something is placed in an environment where dedication and determination and hard work are rewarded?

She becomes consumed.

"When you belong to a minority, you have to be better in order to have the right to be equal."

—Christianne Collage

Maybe it was my personality. I left that womb full of O'Sullivan pride, independence and stubbornness. Add the fact that I knew so many people doubted me and you end up with an eighteen year old girl, away from home, afraid to fail. Before I left for West Point, my boyfriend's father told his American Legion Post 86 pals that I'd be home in a month; that I wouldn't be able to hang physically, that I'd miss his son too much. I was not the stuff that West Point cadets were made of; they knew it. I even knew it. For some very screwy reason, that made me want it more.

They were all looking at us females. The upperclassmen. They didn't think we could hang. They didn't think we belonged. It was up to me to show them. I dwindled down to eighty-five pounds; I gave away a large part of any normalcy I had on R-day; I obsessed with meeting their approval. During Beast, I was in the *Let me show you I deserve to be here just like you* mode.

Every female cadet felt the same way. Most did not go as far as I did to prove themselves; most kept some sort of balance in their lives. It's funny.

On R-Day, I was so glad to see normal girls, but within days, in my quest to be accepted and respected, I drove myself away from normality.

Physical training, called PT, and road marches were the big discriminators. If you wanted the respect of the upperclassmen, you couldn't fall out of either. Labeled "fall outs," most were female, some were male, all were humiliated. I was lucky. The runs, in combat boots, weren't easy for me, but I could complete them—in the same spot in which I started them. This was key. There were different levels of "falling out." Some new cadets lost their place in formation but fell back to run at the rear of the company, the "company stragglers." That was not good, but sure beat falling out and having the other companies, which were running behind yours, pass you. That was like being stood up on prom night after you'd had your hair done and bought a new dress—but stood up by eight hundred guys because that's how many saw you and passed you and labeled you a loser. Right or wrong, at West Point and in the Army, people are judged on their physical fitness ability in a very, very, very big way.

Runs were hard, but for me, road marches were harder. Put a steel pot on my head, a rucksack on my back and a weapon in my hand, and I wore about what I weighed. They sent us out for short day marches first, to build up our strength, but these jaunts through the West Point countryside took every bit of oomph I could muster. The beginning alone, out of the barracks area and straight up the five zillion stone steps to the cadet chapel, was like walking vertically up the side of Mount Everest.

They worked us up gradually to our first bivouac road-march. We marched out to the woods, pitched our little tents (they called them shelter-halves), learned how to use a compass or attack an objective, then marched back to West Point the next afternoon. I'd never slept in the woods in my life. Really. I'd actually only slept outside once in my life in a tent that Fred had borrowed. My outdoor adventure was in my backyard, about five feet away from our den window, with Kim and Sharon, eating Cheetos, drinking Tab, and wondering if the neighborhood boys were listening to us play "Truth or Dare." Not exactly survival training.

At the bivouac site, as Janet and I were pounding our stakes into the ground with our entrenching tools, I was hit with a terrifying thought: Snakes. It dawned on me that we would be sleeping in our sleeping bags, right on the ground. I had never met a snake in my life and had no plans to meet one now. I wondered if Janet had thought about this.

"Hey," I asked her. In the field, the upperclassmen kept to themselves and we could talk freely to our classmates, the one nice thing about going to the field. "What's going to keep snakes out of our tent?"

She looked concerned. Obviously, she hadn't thought about this. She shrugged and we continued to pound the stakes in, putting the shelter-half up and loading our gear inside it. I told her I was going to do something about the snake problem. I looked around, then announced, "Rocks. Let's get some of those rocks and build a little wall around the tent- right where the tent hits the ground. That's where the snakes would slide in."

Janet followed me towards the tree line where we both found good sized rocks, carried them to our tent, and began lining them up. I saw Cadet O'Dowd come out of his shelter half, stand with his hands on his hips, and just watch us. After we had completed a few trips and had lined the base of both sides of the tent with a rock wall about three inches tall, he walked over, shaking his head.

"Ok," he said. "I've got to know." He paused. I wondered how he could be upset with us for trying to protect ourselves. He always seemed to look like he didn't know if he should be mad at me.

He pointed to the rocks. "WHAT are you two doing now?"

"Sir, may I make a statement." I was good.

"Yeah, O'Sullivan. Please do."

In my most concerned voice, full of sincerity, I told him, "Sir, we are building a snake-prevention wall."

The look of disbelief on his face spread into a huge grin and he couldn't hold this one in. He burst out laughing. He walked away towards his tent, but yelled back at us, "You might want to reconsider. Snakes LIKE rocks!"

I looked at Janet and she looked at me. I told her that sounded right. They did like rocks, didn't they? We dismantled the wall. So much for my bright ideas.

**"A cadet will not lie, cheat, or steal,
nor tolerate those who do."**

—Cadet Honor Code, U.S.M.A.

I was *afraid* of runs and road marches, but I was *petrified* of the Honor Code. I didn't lie, cheat, or steal on a regular basis, but there *had* been certain instances here and there...and after our first class on the Honor Code, Seventh Company ("Hellfire and Brimstone, Sir!") stuffed into a classroom listening to an officer listing what "Honor" dictated we could and could not do, I realized that some of the things I'd done before R-day would get me thrown out of West Point. I couldn't think of a more humiliating exit. Not being able to hang physically or flunking calculus would have hurt my pride.

But being thrown out for Honor would have said something about my character. I'd been voted "Character" in the Archbishop Williams National Honor Society! Being thrown out on Honor would not only scar me for life; it would leave an open sore.

I hadn't copied anyone's answers in high school, but I was the willing nerd who let others copy from me and that made me a "Tolerator." Not good. I didn't think I'd ever stolen anything. I'd never lifted anything from Thayer Drug Store or the Stop and Shop. But then the officer talked about all those towels in our bathroom closet back home that said "Holiday Inn" on them. My mother wouldn't have lasted a week at this place. I remembered one trip to West Point to see my brother Paul. The whole crew, Aunt Rita, Uncle Gerard, the cousins, and Nana stopped at a Howard Johnson's on I-84 somewhere in Connecticut. As we got up to leave our table, I looked over to see my seventy-five year old Nana swiping the silverware and putting it in her large Nana Pocketbook. I stared at her. "Nana, what are you doing?"

She replied in her I deserve this. I lived through the Depression and two World Wars way, "We'll need this for the tailgate. They'll never miss it."

In every honor class, I sat petrified. Those genes were in me!

It was me on the phone just a few months ago, in my previous life, telling Peggy that I had to visit my grandmother instead of telling her I just didn't want to go to the plaza with her. I was taught that "White lies" were OK as long as they didn't hurt anyone. Complete integrity was not expected. Being nice was.

Situational Integrity. How we lived our young Catholic lives. The nuns mandated that we go to the sacrament of confession every three weeks. We knew the drill by heart. Kneel in the dark booth, wait for Father to slide the screen back, then begin, "Bless me, Father, for I have sinned. It has been three weeks since my last Confession. I fought with my brother twice. I chewed gum in school twice. I lied once. For these sins and all the sins of my past life, I am very sorry."

Then we thought of a time-saving idea: Skip confession on the third week, go the next week or maybe even the next month, but when we did go, when we were in that dark booth, tell the priest that it had been only three weeks- but add one more lie to our total number of lies. Telling the truth was not as important as Father McCarthy thinking we'd been to confession three weeks ago. It was very confusing. It was better to lie than to hurt someone's feelings. Some lies were OK. But not at West Point.

In some of the lectures we sat through, personal hygiene, first aid, Cadetiquette (how to write thank you notes and use the right fork at banquets in the mess hall), I fell asleep with my eyes open. In Honor classes, I sat up like I had an iron rod jammed up my butt.

The Honor Committee representatives who conducted the classes told us about "pop off" answers, those responses that zapped out of your mouth with no prior thought. They taught us the fine line between tact and honor; it was OK to write a thank you note for the broccoli pie that caused diarrhea. With more knowledge, came more comfort, and my fears gradually subsided.

Sammy. That's what they were saying. But they spelled it S.A. M. I., which stood for Saturday A.M. (or morning) Inspection. What it really meant was standing around and waiting in a hot room for someone to come and inspect in a very anal manner, everything in that hot room. I thought, during my first S.A.M.I, that Sharon and Kim were still asleep. And would be for hours.

Every Saturday, rain or shine, from that first weekend in Beast Barracks through the academic year, someone, not necessarily as nice as your mother, inspected your room, which was supposed to be dust-free, dirt-free and arranged according to the blue cadet regulations book. If your socks were not rolled up properly, if your underwear was not facing the proper way, if there was dust under that English literature book on your bookshelf, the inspecting officer *did* find it. Most inspectors always found *something* and "wrote you up," the term for awarding demerits. Why demerits were "awarded" was like not being able to drink from your water glass. No sense at all. Blue ribbons and prizes are "awarded"; demerits should have been "inflicted" or "de-warded."

It was the night before our first S.A.M.I. and Janet and I were dusting anything that didn't move. We shined the water glass, Ajax'ed the sink, then dried it out (which meant brushing your teeth down the hall in the latrine sinks and for years, still using your hand to scoop water in your mouth because you don't want to get a glass dirty.) We wiped down the baseboards with a damp rag. We moved from the room to our uniforms and we shined the belt buckle, the USMA crest on the hat, shoes and anything not made of cotton, then we set up our white starched belts.

We were shining the bills on our hat, spraying Windex and wiping, when two loud knocks on the door interrupted us. Cadet O'Dowd told us to take our weapons and follow him to his room; we were going to practice Inspection Arms. After the room inspection the next morning, there would be an in-ranks inspection, our first for-grade Inspection Arms. Janet usually got her bolt back, but I still couldn't do it.

It didn't take long for him to see our skills. I wasn't sure if he was frustrated, concerned or angry. I was embarrassed and mad at myself. He took our weapons, told us to go back and finish cleaning our rooms, and come back in ten minutes for the weapons. When we returned ten minutes later, he asked us to try again. I yanked the bolt back on the first try and almost fell over. He smiled and told us to take off.

I wasn't going to ask him, but I figured he had cut our springs. We'd heard through the rumor mill that if the spring was shorter, it was easier to yank that bolt back. This would be the first time I received special compensation because of my sex, or because I was weak, anyway. Later, with more understanding of the big picture, it would bother me. But that night before my first S.A.M.I., concerned only about my own performance, when I pulled that bolt back and did Inspection Arms, I was not bothered one bit. I was ecstatic. I felt bad that I'd had this special treatment, but not bad enough.

Cleaning the room and uniforms was not a big deal for me, but cleaning that weapon was like asking me to explain the Theory of Relativity. Janet and I could take the M-14 apart and use the little cleaning kit we were issued to wipe down the various parts, but we had no idea what a clean housing assembly should look like. We lay the parts that we thought we'd cleaned -we'd rubbed cloth on them anyway- on our beds, then we put the weapon back together again. After we cleaned it, we looked down the bore, expecting to see what, I don't know. We just hoped for the best.

The waiting was torture. You hadn't slept much the night before, cleaning past Taps illegally by flashlight, worrying about whatever it was you hadn't done right, knowing it was something, then finally, laying softly on top of the bed, dozing in and out, sweating from the ninety degree heat and humidity. After breakfast, you ping back to your room, put the finishing touches on it, one more sweep, one more wipe. The wait begins. It wasn't as if you could be watching Saturday morning cartoons while you waited. No radio, no stereo, no TV, no Mr. Coffee. With nothing to do but worry, you wondered: Who will inspect? The highest ranking inspecting officer was the Commandant of Cadets, a one-star general in the Army, known as the "Comm." Chances were slim that he'd be around, but you could still worry about it. During Beast, the commander of New Cadet Basic Training was a colonel who served as a regimental tactical officer (RTO) during the academic year. Chances of getting him were slim as well, but who knows?

The list of potential inspectors was endless. The company tactical officer, known as the "Tac," was a commissioned officer, a captain or major in the Army, who was responsible for the health and welfare of each cadet in the company. Back in the '70s, some Tacs were very visible; some were not. If you didn't get the Tac, you'd end up with someone from the cadet chain of command. There was the company commander, the platoon leader, the platoon sergeant, and everyone's brother. Not a snowball's chance in Hell that someone would wander by and say, "Sorry, we have run out of inspectors today. Relax, use your water glass and take a nap."

The results of a room inspection were very dependent upon the personalities of the inspectors. If the inspector was really into it, he'd pick up every thing that was not nailed down, eye-ball it, hold it up to the light and when he turned around, you'd want to tape a sign on his back that said "Kick me. I'm an asshole." If the inspector wasn't really into it, he might ask you where you're from and then talk about the Red Sox while he gazes over your stuff and says "pretty good room." Very few cadets had mastered the art of inspecting without being jerks. Leadership was hard when it was about the dumb stuff, like water spots in the sink. An interesting phenomenon occurred with cadet inspectors who had been picked on as new cadets. Peculiarly, cadets who had abysmal plebe years were more revengeful, less sympathetic. Another phenomenon was related to breakfast cereal. There were ten little boxes at the table in the mess hall, but only one of each flavor so if two people wanted Lucky Charms, one ended up with Wheat Chex. You had to hope your inspector got his favorite cereal. You also had to hope he hadn't just been dumped by his girlfriend. That was *never* good.

Knock, knock.

"Enter, Sir."

An entourage wearing the white over grey uniform, white starched shirts with grey trousers, entered my room for my first ever S.A.M.I. It was the platoon leader, a big guy named Sullivan with a crew cut and mean eyes, followed by the platoon sergeant, a football player named Genatossio with a notebook and pen in hand. Cadet O'Dowd brought up the rear.

"Sir, New Cadet O'Sullivan reports." My name was alphabetically ahead of Janet's so I got to do the reporting.

And then I inhale. Hold that breath while he holds up the water glass. Water stains, he says. Cadet Genatossio, acting scribe for the inspector, writes it down. *I don't think Genatossio likes me. I think he may be a male chauvinist pig. No way*, I think. *I cleaned that thing.* I'm still inhaling. He looks at the shoes in the closet. He looks in the drawer under the wardrobe and bends over. *Oh, no. Not good.* The bending over can't be good. I'm still inhaling. He grabs the bag of oat bran and I hear him mutter under his breath. He says to the platoon sergeant, "Unauthorized food in room."

I think to myself, *If I were going to have unauthorized food in my room, I'd have gone for Devil Dogs.* I see Cadet O'Dowd signal for the platoon sergeant.

"O'Sullivan needs that kitty litter," he says with his New Jersey no-nonsense much too loud voice, "It's for medicinal purposes."

They confer, but they do this quietly so I can't hear. The platoon leader looks at me, with pity, I think; I'm still at attention and still inhaling. He shakes his head. He looks at the platoon sergeant and says, "Delete that." Phew. He checks out the socks in the dresser drawer. If I exhale, I'm sure he'll find something wrong. He looks at us and says, "Pretty good room."

Move my bed and look at how clean the baseboard is, I think. Still inhaling. He turns around and walks out, followed by the platoon sergeant. Behind his back, Cadet O'Dowd gives us a thumbs-up, then follows them out of the room. Exhale. Phew. A little embarrassing to know that the upperclassmen now all know I live primarily in a constipated state, but I'll get over it; too busy to worry with the in-ranks inspection on deck.

We peeked out the door to make sure the coast was clear, then we darted, 180 steps per minute, straight across the hall from our door to the wall. Pinging, eyes straight ahead, we hooked a left turn at the doorway to the latrine, and ducked inside. We raced back to our room, put our white starched belts on, trying to figure out where the buckle goes, without touching it and getting smudge marks on it. We grabbed our white gloves and our weapons and were about to run out the door to the formation downstairs when Mark, the prepster burst through our door.

Prepsters are great. Mark knew we were clueless and came over to help. He asked if we'd run plastic wrap down our bore of our weapon, something about the saran wrap getting dust out, but I really wasn't listening. I'd do whatever anyone told me to do. We panicked. We were supposed to be at formation before the minute callers started calling the ten-minute bell. Janet took the piece of Saran wrap on the weapons cleaning rod that Mark left us and rammed it down her weapon. She tossed it to me and ran out the door. I rammed it down my weapon, flipped the light switch off, and followed her out the door.

We stood in ranks out in the hot July sun trying not to move. *If I keep thinking about this itch, it will not go away, so I will think about something else. Like the drip of sweat slowly working its way from my mashed hair trickling down my face, causing zits to erupt along the way, down my neck, scorching from the sun, and now into my undershirt. How many things this guy is finding wrong with the guy standing in the squad ahead of me. Will he just move on for crying out loud? I should be practicing my knowledge. How's the cow? Sir, she walks...*

It was about a century before he got to me, a very hot century. He stood in front of me. I whipped up my weapon and did Inspection Arms. He grabbed the weapon out of my hand like a rude two year old grabbing a toy from another kid. Cadet O'Dowd had warned us that some inspecting officers will try to knock us over with that grab. I tried hard not to jerk back, but knew that I did. He looked at my weapon. I was looking into his lower chest, at attention with my eyes straight ahead and that put my big brown eyes at somewhere above belt buckle level, but I could feel his head shaking. He tossed the weapon to Cadet Genatossio who was next to him. He looked down the barrel and shook his head. This is not a good sign, I think. Cadet Genatossio tossed it to Cadet O'Dowd. I couldn't see him, but I had a feeling his head was shaking, too.

The platoon leader announced loudly so most of New York could hear, "Plastic down the barrel of the weapon." He didn't add "the Idiot's weapon", but he may as well have. Apparently, when I yanked that cleaning rod out of my rifle, the saran wrap had remained behind. My first In-Ranks Inspection closed with a thud.

I met my first Army family that second Sunday of Beast. I'd never met an Army family before. Each new cadet was assigned a family who lived on post, four cadets per family. I stood in the parking lot across from the barracks with two male cadets and one other female cadet when Captain Mulligan introduced himself, then loaded us in his station wagon and drove us up a long winding hill to his brick house. Mrs. Mulligan was blond and pretty, from outside Boston, which I thought was so cool, and their three young daughters were blond and adorable. I sat on their plaid couch and smiled for the first time in weeks.

It didn't dawn on me that the females were in pairs for safety reasons. The other female cadet with me was a woman, really. She'd been to college, spoke almost eloquently and oozed with self-confidence. When Mrs. Mulligan asked us what we wanted to drink and she asked for a glass of wine, my eyes bugged out. My mother drank wine. I had desperation in my voice when I asked if they had any Tab. I was addicted and needed a tasteless swig bad.

I heard Captain Mulligan talking to his wife and saw her look at me, then smile. She asked, "Gail, did your father call up here before R-Day and ask if he should be concerned about your weight?"

How'd they know? I told her Yes, Ma'am, he did. She laughed, then explained, "My husband works in admissions. Your father spoke to him. He had no idea what to tell your father so he put him on hold and called me at home. I couldn't think of anything but bananas!" What a coincidence. It was the first time I heard "What a small Army this is."

I didn't want to go back to the barracks. Wine Woman didn't either. Misery enjoys company and I was glad to learn that I wasn't the only one not having a good time at this thing called Beast.

"Ambition is so powerful a passion in the human breast, that however high we reach, we are never satisfied."

—Niccolo Machiavelli

Weight was a worry. And would be a worry for a long time. Before West Point would give me an appointment, I had to take the physical, like all the other applicants, given by the Department of Defense medical review board. I was deemed physically not qualified for admission. I was underweight and I didn't have enough teeth.

Dr. Leigh, the pediatrician I'd had for eighteen years, wrote a letter stating that although I weighed five pounds below the weight requirement for my height (at sixty-four inches I had to weigh 103 pounds; I'd been a solid ninety-seven pounds for about four years), I was as healthy as a horse. I'd been her biggest baby, my mother exclaimed. West Point waived the weight requirement. Dr. Brackett, our dentist, wrote a letter stating that the teeth had never come in, that I'd never got wisdom teeth or back molars, but it would not in any way hinder my performance. West Point waived the teeth requirement.My father worried about the weight requirement. A week before I was supposed to report at West Point, he learned that they weighed the candidates on R-Day, so he called the admissions office to make sure they wouldn't send me home because I was short those five pounds. I knew he'd called because when he got off the phone, he told me to eat bananas. I said, "What?" "Eat bananas," My father responded, like this was a perfectly natural thing to do.

"I don't really like bananas, Dad."

"I don't care. The man said Eat Bananas."

I didn't eat bananas. I went to Dairy Queen and ate peanut butter parfaits and went to Valle's Steak House and ate cream puffs. I felt sick. I felt like a whale. I still weighed only ninety-nine pounds on R-Day. No one seemed to care. I was shuffled off to the next station and my weight became a non-concern. For a while anyway.

My weight went from a non-issue in high school, to an issue before R-Day, to more of an issue during Beast. And there it stayed, as an issue, for years.

It was an innocent remark by Cadet O'Dowd that did it. He didn't mean it, for sure. We were leaving the mess hall after a dinner of Salisbury steak and mashed potatoes, green beans and dinner rolls, and I was walking at attention down the wide aisles squeezed in between hundreds of other new cadets reeking of sweat and gravy when Cadet O'Dowd chanced to be next to me. He looked down at me and said, like What a Nice Day or How about them Yankees, "You'd better watch it, O'Sullivan."

I didn't respond. I didn't know what he was talking about. He went on, "The women in the Class of '80 got real serious Hudson Hips Disease."

"Yes, Sir," I dutifully responded. I figured he meant that they all gained weight. Food was all over the tables in the mess hall, everything from bread and peanut butter to chocolate sheet cake, although most new cadets spent more time looking at all of it than eating any of it. Cadet O'Dowd was a table commandant who liked to eat and believed in letting us eat as well. Maybe he thought I'd get fat.

He couldn't have realized what a nutritional ninny I was. The girls in high school had gone through diet stages where they ate only carrots, but I didn't do vegetables. I didn't do anything green or orange, and stuck mostly to chocolate and Fritos. Despite my heavy input of garbage, I hovered constantly between ninety-seven and ninety-nine pounds, born blessed in the metabolism department.

But Cadet O'Dowd, my god, told me I could get fat. So I did what I thought I had to do to avoid the Hudson Hips Disease. I cut all fats and starches from my diet. I drank only water, not fruit punch or juices. If we had hamburgers for lunch, I ate the meat patty, the lettuce and tomato, skipped the bun and the dessert. It wasn't even hard for me. This new eating was just an extension of the very disciplined and regimented way of life I was leading. I didn't even think about it. It was like waking up early for PT or learning my knowledge. It was all part of being a good cadet.

I didn't stop eating. I never purged. For the first time in my life, I ate only healthy foods but had minimal, if any, fat in my diet. This is highly recommended if you're thirty pounds overweight. But if you're weighing in at less than one hundred pounds soaking wet and you're exerting more calories on a daily basis than you'd ever exerted before in your life, you will land in Emaciated Land, where I ended up. I looked pitiful, but didn't realize it. I knew I wasn't fat, but had no idea how thin I was. When people told me, I didn't listen. Before long, I could have been posing for CARE commercials.

Female cadets came in all sizes. Some large, some medium, a few small, some accordions, who went in and then out, from rail thin to tubby, plump-faced, then back to thin again. The accordions spent a lot of time at the tailor's having their uniforms altered.

In Beast, we learned the Basics. Eating Disorders 101. We can't fail. We can't get fat. Biting, angry comments about the women in the Class of '80 or gentle, concerned warnings about the gobs of calories on the mess hall tables- It all boiled down to one rule, one road to respect: Don't Get Fat.

Fear of Fat, perhaps, or maybe a power thing or maybe just stress relief, led to Closet Eating. I don't want you to see me Eat, so I won't Eat in front of you. I want you to think I don't Eat! Then you'll like me! Or maybe we were saying: I have the Power! I have Control! I will eat until my heart is content and my stomach is overflowing and what can You do about it? You can't do anything about it! But I can purge! And the Purgers, after downing buckets of Haagan Daz and Chips Ahoy, retched in the latrines after Taps.

Whatever size we were, we all wanted the same thing. We wanted to please. We wanted to belong.

I didn't know how thin I was, and it didn't happen overnight. From R-Day through my first two years, I lost eight pounds, not much compared to many male cadets, but a lot when it comes off a small frame. I ignored my roommate's concerns, my mother's questions. I denied myself pleasurable food because I thought that was part of playing the game. Food, never a big deal to me, just became way less important. The path I thought was marked "Good Cadet" was in the opposite direction of the path marked "Normal"—and I marched down it, thin, dumb and happy.

"When faith is lost, when honor dies; the man is dead."

—John Greenleaf Whittier

It was hard to remember who you were before Beast. Mass helped. I never missed a Sunday mass growing up and walked with Sharon to daily mass during Lent, but no mass was ever as important as Wednesday night masses during Beast. The "fish eaters" formed up on the apron, the cement area between the barracks and the plain, and an upper-class "fish eater" marched us to the Catholic chapel, perched on a grassy hill overlooking the Hudson. Its' stone façade was deceiving; warmth enveloped the pews and inside, sitting among our classmates, we were authorized to relax. Inside that chapel, I was the girl I was before R-Day, except I wore a strange get-up and was much uglier. Mass was the only single event in my new life that I had done back in Braintree.

After, we had cookies and juice. We talked to each other, squeezed together in the basement of the chapel, wet grass on the soles of our shoes, fresh pimples where the camouflage on our faces had been scrubbed off. I saw Patty, Jimmy and Mike who were also in a sort of Beast Shock. I saw Bill, whom I'd met at a dinner in high school for students who were going to West Point. He was in my Beast Company, and always looked at me like "you're still here?" The new cadets from Massachusetts gravitated towards each other. Lots of hockey players, Bob, Matt, Ed, Digger. These were the kind of guys I grew up with. Oreos, Tang, hockey players from home, and a little religion to boot, Wednesday night chapel was the only relief Beast offered. In a world where duty was everything, spirituality, which had always been a duty for me, became less of a duty, more of an escape, a relief, a comfort. If I'd had time to think about it, I would have put it together: When duty becomes important to you, it's not a chore.

First family visit and picnic by the Hudson River during Beast Barracks: (*left to right*) Jim McConville, Gail, Patty Mahoney, Mike McGrath. August 1977

five

I'll See You in September

Just when we were used to what we had, we got a new everything. New squad leader, new platoon sergeant, new platoon leader, new stress level. It was the third Saturday in Beast and it was "Change of Detail." After our parade in the morning, we stood under Patton, a mammoth green soldier, who, back in the '70s glared into the windows of the old cadet library. It was here that we'd say good-bye to Cadet O'Dowd.

"Gunga Din", he called me. I'd never seen the movie. We were on one of those road marches I dreaded, marching up an endless hill, all rocks and gravel, behind the ski slope, and I started to fall back. It happened too quickly. The hill became a cliff, its steepness catching me off guard. My helmet, that steel pot slicking my buzz-cut to my head with sweat, crept down over my eyes and kept me from seeing anything but gray stones and dirt. I continued to climb, but I felt someone next to me. It was Dave, the guy behind me in the squad. I was falling out.

Before Dave could pass me, Cadet O'Dowd appeared from the back of the squad. His face was soaked with sweat; he was beet red. He didn't have a pore on his body that didn't perspire poolfuls.

"You all right?"

I couldn't look up. Just kept putting those legs in front of the other and said, "Yes, Sir."

He shook his head and said to me, "You can do this, O'Sullivan."

My legs kept moving. "I'll try, Sir."

He called me Gunga-Din from then on. I had no idea who or what Gunga-Din was, so he explained the famous line "I'll try, Sir" at the next assembly area. He knew that I was crushed. I'd caught back up to Dave over the top of that hill, but was still angry, embarrassed and just devastated. Many leaders crush harder once you're already crushed, but O'Dowd didn't work that way. Either he knew what to do to motivate me or he was afraid I'd cry.

I knew I'd miss him. Dave and Jeff were together, away by themselves, and Jeff held a brown paper bag behind his back. They had asked us all for money to chip in and buy him something but I never figured it would be alcohol. Jeff had asked a friend who was coming to visit to buy it for him, and he made a formal presentation of the bottle of Jack Daniels to our first detail Beast squad leader. Cadet O'Dowd seemed to be as shocked as I was, but he grinned fast and laughed. He couldn't wait to get to the beach.

He told us he'd See Us In September. The cadre had driven us nuts all week singing the lyrics to that old tune. At Patton, when we said good bye to Cadet O'Dowd, I got all choked up, but I cry at the *Sound of Music*. The guys didn't seem to be as affected as I was by it all.

That afternoon, the change of detail day, they called it, we could have our first visitors. My parents were driving up and bringing Sean with them. After we said good-bye to Cadet O'Dowd, I went to look for them, near the chain from where they had watched me on R-Day. I was excited about seeing them, anxious about seeing Sean, proud that I was still at West Point, nervous about the new detail. We couldn't show Public Displays of Affection, or PDA, but I was never much of a public displayer anyway. My mother was and she hugged me hard; even my dad got into the act. But I just stood there, like a dweeb in my white starched shirt tucked into my gray pants, with my geeky black shoes and my silly hat, looking at Sean. He looked good. He had on jeans and a t-shirt; his hair was longer than mine. What's wrong with this picture, I thought.

I wasn't a very good feminist. I wasn't comfortable with this whole role-reversal thing. Had Sean been the cadet and I'd been the girlfriend, fine. It was too weird being the one in uniform at a military academy and having him home at a normal school. I felt awkward and uncomfortable. He could care less. He didn't say anything about the mailman's hat or the nun shoes. He acted normal, talking about home, who was doing what and who was working where. But I was having those *That was then, This is Now* flashbacks. I was so eager, so ready, to step into the future. I didn't have the time or energy to worry about the past; I didn't want it back there calling me, teasing me to return to it. Sean and I didn't even kiss during that Saturday visit. We weren't alone anywhere we could have. This is going out?

Cadet Rook was a twit. He couldn't compare to O'Dowd. Rook was very strict, very professional, with zero personality and not an inkling of charisma. I didn't *not* like him, but I didn't like him either. He didn't appear to like me much either, which hurt my feelings, but since he didn't appear to like any of us, I still got to sleep at night.

His roommate, our "sister" squad leader, filled the gaps, and there were lots, missing in Rook's leadership. Cadet Ulmer was a year behind Cadet Rook, one of the few members of the second class, the cows, who had been chosen to be a Beast squad leader. He had a sense of humor and interjected sarcasm whenever he could. It was almost as if he knew Rook was a twit and we needed him. And we did.

> **"He that respects himself is safe from others;**
> **He wears a coat of mail that none can pierce."**
>
> **—Henry Wadsworth Longfellow**

In the list of "Things to leave at home when reporting to West Point", they should have added Self-Esteem. And for me, they should have added "Looks." It wasn't as if I was a knock-out on R-Day, but by mid-Beast, my looks had taken a serious nose-dive, spiraling daily into the land of no return. The haircuts had put the nail in the coffin.

I had escaped the R-Day trip to the barbershop because my adorable Dorothy Hamill bob that I got a week before R-day back home in the real world, was within regulations, though I know that intensely aggravated the upperclassman who told me. It seemed like they wanted us to look bad, maybe so they could better rationalize not liking us? All the new cadets were marched to the barber shop weekly. Back then, there was one female hairstylist, but who had time to wait for her to be free? When my first trip to the barber came a week into Beast, I ended up in the chair of Big Ed who had obviously not had much practice trimming cute little bobs. He picked up a razor blade. I stared. It was just a blade, no handle. A single, sharp, silver blade. I wasn't sure what I was supposed to do. Jump out of the chair? Yell? I stared some more and just sat. He attacked my hair like a lunatic with a weed-whacker, leaving me with but an inch of hair on my head. I looked like Gomer Pyle. I refused to cry until I got back to my room and then I let it rip.

Janet and I figured that our looks were part of the sacrifice, but we didn't like it. The farmer's tan didn't help any. Our arms were block tanned, with our upper arms not even seeing the light from the refrigerator and our lower arms bronzed. The fatigue caps left a permanent crease in our upper fore-heads, the steel pots left "helmet head", a sweaty wave of hair that sunk into our scalps. There weren't many female officers around, but the ones we did see hadn't just posed for the cover of Cosmo. Captain White was infamous for her lipstick, a fire engine red shade, visible for miles. This would be us?

We were out on a bivouac, had pitched our tents and just finished the dinner rations, hot A's they were called, sticky rice and mystery meat, soupy corn and a poor mimic of cake. Cadet Ulmer walked over towards Janet and me and waved us to follow him. He'd heard us talking, he told us, and wanted to show us something.

We walked through the woods in silence for about ten minutes. Janet and I didn't know what was going on, but we were used to doing things for unknown reasons, so we kept walking. Further out in the woods, we could see two figures up ahead, beneath the trees, talking. As we got closer, we saw two female cadets, wearing the tan khaki uniform, which only upperclass-men could wear. Plebes were not issued it. It was a very cool uniform, tan shirt, tucked in neatly with khaki pants. One girl was tall, blond, blue-eyed. The other had dark hair and eyes. They were the most attractive girls we'd seen since R-Day. I felt dirty and homely near them. It took me a few sec-onds to register that the brunette was Danna, the girl Patty and I had met light years ago on our visit with Billy, the rabble-rouser. The girls didn't say much; Cadet Ulmer told us they were yearlings and had walked out from Buckner to see us. They felt awkward, being on display for us, but they smiled and encouraged us before we went one way and they went the other. They didn't need to say a word. Just seeing them was enough. There was hope. They looked so normal.

"Prejudices, it is well known, are most difficult to eradicate from the heart whose soil has never been loosened or fertilized by education, they grow there, firm as weeds among rocks."

— Charlotte Bronte

My looks ended up bringing my self-esteem down to rock bottom. I think it was my looks anyway. I can't help but think that if I had been a six feet three, all-county wide receiver, Cadet Rook would not have pulled me aside one night in the field. Our squad was sitting more or less together on a huge boulder, cleaning our weapons, with little containers of oil and tiny brushes on our laps. He called me. Just me. The 5'3", ninety-seven-pound weakling.

"O'Sullivan!" It didn't sound good. It had been decided, he informed me, just me, that I would "move out" first thing in the morning to go to the qualification range a day earlier than the rest of the company. No sugar coating with this guy. He looked at me and he saw DUD painted all over me; he had no trouble telling me I was a "potential Bolo."

Bolo meant that you did not qualify with your weapon. This was like not getting your license on your fifteenth road test. Soldiers had to qualify with their personal weapons as part of the Soldier Deal; it was like saluting and saying "sir." There were different levels of qualification, so it wasn't impossible to do. Depending upon how many targets you hit, you could be an Expert, a Sharpshooter, a Marksman. Bolos were none of the above. Bolos shot at passing airplanes or tunnels that led beneath the ground to China. The hierarchy decided I was a Bolo. Making me feel good about myself was not on their list of things to do on summer vacation.

There were only a few of us from Seventh Company, Hellfire and Brimstone, Sir. We sat in the back of the truck, dejected, the losers, being bounced up and down the gravel road to the range to join 6th Company who was already out there. They figured if we didn't qualify with this company, we could then join our company when it was their turn the next day, and try again. This made not making the junior varsity cheerleading squad in ninth grade seem trivial. I jumped down from that truck, knowing that I had a huge L for Loser stamped on my forehead. And I was mad. Cadet Rook had some nerve; calling me aside in front of everyone and making me feel like such a dud. I had never really thought much of him, but that morning at the range, without my squad, with the other losers in 7th Company; I thought Rook was a real jerk.

It seemed that for every real jerk, there was a counter-jerk. At the range, there was a cadet-in-charge, called a C-I-C. This was no surprise since during Beast there was a C-I-C of everything from Blisters to Chapel. This C-I-C was one of the good ones. Cadet Aquino ran the instruction, first the lecture in the sun soaked bleachers, then the firing down on the range. Professional but kind, he didn't make us feel like the losers we thought we were. I liked shooting the M-16. I qualified as a sharpshooter and couldn't wait for Rook to find out.

He never said a word to me about it.

Being singled out was never good. I wanted to blend in, to be like liquid and just flow through the cracks, smoothly and easily, just be a regular cadet. I didn't like to make waves in high school, before I was one of the 200 women out of 4,000 cadets at West Point. Bringing attention to me now was the last thing on earth I wanted to do. So when all the women had to go into Thayer Hall for a lecture one hot afternoon late in Beast, I was perturbed.

Sitting in an auditorium with all my female classmates, no males, no upperclassmen, doors closed, was weird. I felt odd. There was something neat about it. The speaker was a civilian woman, Dr. Peterson from the Department of Physical Education, and she was going to talk about purely female things. She showed us a movie of the women in the Class of '80, clips from their Beast and their plebe year. "There's a New Kid in Town," a '70s song by the Eagles was playing in the background. (I hear that song thirty years later and think of the Women in the Class of 1980.) Dr. Peterson told us that we probably would experience irregularity in our periods. I didn't worry about it. I'd never been regular, so this was nothing new to me. Then she told us that we should see her immediately if we thought we might be pregnant. Huh? I thought. Pregnant? Was I missing something here? I didn't even kiss my boyfriend on the one day this summer I saw him. How the heck could someone get pregnant here?

You sure can miss a lot when you live in your own little bubble.

The Best Week Of Your Life, the upperclassmen said. They'd been ranting and raving about Lake Frederick for weeks, and though they tried to make it sound like some sort of a mini-Jamaican vacation, I didn't buy it. Something about lying on the sand with your M-16 firmly attached to your hip took all the fun out of this resort. Plus, I was scared to death about the road march out to the lake. It was our longest march, fourteen miles, and this little Gunga-Din didn't know if she could hang.

Before we left for Frederick, they posted the company assignments for the academic year. They hung a computer printout in the hallway across from the orderly room listing each new cadet's name, alphabetically ordered, and the new academic company. Beast companies were numbered 1-8. Academic year companies were divided into four regiments and within each regiment, there were companies A-I. There were thirty-six total academic companies and when we marched back from Lake Frederick, Beast would be in our rear-view mirror and we'd march into our new academic year company. We would leave 7th Company, our friends, our roommates. Just to add a little excitement to the stress level, we'd also be inundated by upperclassmen. During Beast, in a company of about 150 new cadets, there was one upperclassman for every five new cadets. In the academic year company, we could look forward to maybe three upperclassmen for every one new cadet. Not good. If I made the road march back, that was what I had to look forward to. More of them.

I found O'Sullivan below O'Shaughnessy on the roster. I was going to Company F-2. "The Zoo."

No one else from my Beast squad was going to F-2, but, lucky new cadet that I was, my company training officer was a "Zoo member": Cadet Disher.

Second detail had arrived and I'd heard about Disher the Dick and I'd seen him yelling at some of my company-mates, but I didn't meet him until later. Jeff had hurt his leg and was on crutches. He'd be going out to the field for our overnight bivouac in the sick call truck, the "meat wagon" for the "sick, lame and lazy." The night before the road march, when Janet and I were packing our stuff, Jeff "pinged" over to our room, on crutches, and asked us if we wanted to put any of our stuff in his rucksack. That would lighten our load. Nice of him to ask; made perfect sense to me. We gave him our shelter halves, tent poles and stakes.

A shelter half was an ingenious invention. Each person got a half; you snapped the two halves together, staked them in, popped up the sides with the stakes, and you had one pup tent which two cadets shared. It poured buckets the day of our road march, all day, no breaks in the rain, constant downpour. West Point does not cancel road marches due to rain. When we got to the bivouac site, everyone splashed in the mud, putting up their tents in a hurry. Janet and I looked at each other: There was no sick call truck in sight. We stood dejected, two drowned rats, exhausted, sopping, shivering and miserable with no tent to put up.

Disher spotted us and *lit into us,* as they say. Up and down, in and out, yelling so hard he almost choked on his anger, screaming phrases like "Dicking on your classmates", "Can't carry your own load", "Don't belong here." With our equipment drenched into our backs and the downpour seeping under our steel pots, this guy really knew how to motivate us.

And so, when I stood reading the company rosters outside that orderly room, Disher walked up behind me and barked into my ear, just to make sure I knew he was going to be my shadow all year long. I could not believe that this jerk would be in my company. I not only had that road march to look forward to, I had a year of Disher, too. My shoulders sagged and I felt like crying. I turned to walk back to my room and saw Cadet Damsel. I'd never talked to Cadet Damsel, but he was one of the "fish-eaters" who marched us to Wednesday night mass. He was a quiet guy with eyes that poked out of his head and I'd seen him talk to new cadets, going up to them and speaking into their ears, almost softly, so no one else would hear. I was half-way down the hall, the orderly room and Disher behind me, when Cadet Damsel called me, "New Cadet O'Sullivan, halt."

I stopped. He came over and stood about a foot away, talking quietly in a conversational voice. "I'm in F-2, New Cadet O'Sullivan. Don't worry. You'll do fine. Keep up the good work."

One of the West Point Laws of Physics: For every jerk, there was one and only one counter-jerk.

Moving to F-2 meant getting a new roommate and this was a humungous worry for me. The guys didn't seem to worry so much about their roommates, but for me, it was all I thought about. I'd be able to meet her before the march out. We moved, via our new cadet backs, anything that was not going with us to Lake Frederick to the new rooms we'd live in when we returned from our week at the lake. I loaded my huge green duffel bag with uniforms, toilet articles, shoes and hats, put it on my back, walked down the three flights of stairs, against the wall, eyes straight ahead, across Central Area at 180 steps per minute, up the five flights of stairs, against the wall, eyes straight ahead, and into my new room in F-2. The new room faced a big stone wall. What a view. I dumped my stuff on the bed, put it away, then went back out, down the five flights of stairs, against the wall, eyes straight ahead, across Central Area at 180 steps per minute, up the three flights of stairs to my "old" room to load my empty green duffel bag with more stuff. All over the area, new cadets were crouched behind big green duffel bags, moving into their new rooms.

After the second trip, tired, hot and thirsty, I peeked into my new roommate's closet and checked out her shoes. They were small, smaller than mine. I read her name on her uniforms: "West." *Is that Irish, I thought?* It didn't sound familiar. Our trips into the room kept missing each other, just like on R-Day. *Do they do this on purpose?* In their instructions, it must have read: *Add stress to the new cadet by insuring he/she does not meet his/her roommate until the last possible moment.* At least her shoes were small. That was a good sign. I'd been lucky to have Janet for a roommate. I'd met some of the other girls and there were some odd ducks out there. I wondered if they said the same thing about me. I wasn't very worldly, but I surmised that some of these girls *liked* other girls. Though I knew it wasn't very Christ-like of me, I didn't want a big girl who liked other girls for my roommate.

For the third time in an hour, I heaved my duffel bag onto the bed and struggled to disengage myself from the straps when the door opened and in shuffled a short redhead, whose duffel bag was longer than she was tall. I sighed, got my duffel bag off my back, and smiled. Not an Amazon.

We began the small talk that females do. How are you doing, how much have you moved in, what company are you in, where are you from in real life.

"West Point," she replied.

I was confused.

"West Point?" I asked. "People live here?"

She looked at me like I was simple, and responded, "My father is in the Army."

"Oh," I said, remembering the Mulligans and all the brick houses in their neighborhood that must have been lived in by other people in the Army. "What's he do?"

She looked uncomfortable. I suddenly made the connection. My eyes opened wide. "Colonel Arvid E. West, Jr.? The commander of Cadet Basic Training? I memorized his name!"

She nodded.

"Wow," I said, "My father works for the phone company."

I didn't tell her that I'd never heard the name Arvid before.

I didn't fall out on the march out to Lake Frederick and had a whole week to worry about whether or not I'd make the march back in to the barracks. We set up our shelter halves, over 1,200 of them, dress right dress, like the desks in Sister Agnesca's classroom, on the grassy fields near the lake.

Our days were crammed with military training. We learned how to identify terrain features, *I thought a saddle was for a horse*, navigate with a compass and a map, *can't I just follow the guys in front of me*, fight with pugil sticks and thrust a bayonet, *I will be dead two minutes into a war*. I played the game, never thinking about it. I never thought that I'd have to do a buttstroke to someone's head. I was just trying to get through each day. Besides, women wouldn't do this in war, would they? I didn't know what women did in war. I didn't even know what *men* did in war; I should have watched more war movies. I figured women wouldn't be doing typing, or the feminists would have a conniption fit, but I didn't think we'd be "fixing bayonets" either.

Over the summer, I realized that listening to my father and brother and understanding their feelings about women at West Point gave me an advantage. I didn't necessarily believe that West Point should remain all-male. But I did understand that, like my father and my brother, many, many, *many* people felt otherwise and whether they were right or wrong, these feelings, *these very passionate feelings*, existed. Since my first word was "please" and writing thank you notes was a hobby of mine, it's no earth shattering surprise that my reaction to all this was a polite one. I believed women should walk on eggshells. I thought we should *gently* break down the walls of prejudice one cadet at a time. I thought we should march into the ranks of history without making too much noise. I thought, *Give me a chance to convince you that I can do this.*

The last night at Frederick was the big talent show. I don't know who had talents but the whole class would sit on the hillside and watch the show. It was a break, relaxing on the grass, watching our classmates who actually thought they could sing and dance. Janet and I were waiting to march down the hill to the stage; we were sitting outside our tent, shining our boots, when I saw Patty walking toward us. She was with an upperclassman, dressed in his khakis. We both hopped up to attention when they came over to us. It was Billy, the rabble-rouser, and he greeted me smiling, "I can't believe that you're still here! It's good to see you."

He told us he was here for the talent show; the rabble-rousers put on a rally before the show. He said he hoped we'd join the rabble-rousers when the school year started. After six weeks of being good at absolutely nothing, it was nice to be wanted. He could have told us he wanted us to join his manure-stomping club and we'd have asked when the first meeting was. We watched the rally that night and got excited about being real college cheerleaders.

Little did we know.

I made the march back from Frederick, but barely. The march-back was at the end of the hardest things I'd ever done in my life, physically and mentally, but it was just the beginning of another chapter of a *different* kind of hard. We marched with our company onto the cement area in front of the mess hall, dropped our gear, marched into the mess hall and ate our last meal with our beast squad. Emotions were on overdrive. I was apprehensive, sad, uncertain, and scared to death. Most of all, I was disgustingly dirty and dying to take a shower.

six

Welcome to the Zoo

"I have been searching history to see if really a woman has any precedent to claim the right to have her rights, and I am compelled to say that we men are not so much ahead of any women after all, and the only way we have kept our reputation up is by keeping her down—and don't you forget it."

-George Foster, 1886

The Class of 1979 got a bad rep. During Beast, our squad leaders were mostly firsties, seniors in the Class of '78, but during the academic year, the squad leaders were all cows from the Class of '79. These squad leaders were members of the last class to graduate from West Point as an all-male class, the "Last Class With Balls," so they said. (I don't know who said; *they* just said.) Supposedly some even had the letters "LCWB" inscribed on their rings, but I've never asked anyone and I don't really want to know. I'd be embarrassed for them if they showed me.

The Class of 1980 held their twentieth reunion in the fall of 2000 and I listened to some of them rake the Class of '79 over the coals. I thought of Ulmer, Kardos, Martin and Noll, and I almost stood up and came to their defense, but still twenty years later, I remained ball-less. Plus, these women were doing some serious venting and I figured I'd let them get it off their chest. '79 got a bad rep because of a few bad apples, loud-mouths, idiots, dicks.

In F-2, we had some great cows. They breathed professionalism; they were good, funny, concerned. Unfortunately, there were at least two, perhaps more, who passed Jerk in the second grade and were well on their way to Asshole Land. Amazing how the immature few can give the whole class a bad name.

I left my beast squad on the apron, sad to say good bye but glad to leave Beast behind; and, I marched my tired, sweaty body up to the fifth floor of F-2. My squad leader came by the room, Cadet Howard, a normal, average guy, trying to get by, trying to graduate. He had that same look Cadet O'Dowd used to have: the *what do I make of her?* look. There were four plebes in his squad, the affirmative action squad. Two black guys, both would turn out to be great guys, and two females. Linda was nowhere to be found. Cadet Howard told me she was in the hospital and I'd better unpack and get our room squared away. All the plebes were meeting with the Tac in an hour in the company day room.

They called this Re-Orgy Week, short for Re-organization. It was not fun. The upperclassmen lurked in the halls, having no life, just waiting for us plebes to wander outside our door. My self-esteem was up and down like a fiddler's elbow. Feel pretty good about making the march back from Frederick. Up. Feel bad when someone screams, "You call that a dress-off? You shine your shoes with a candy bar?" Down. Feel good when you get mail from home and your mother tells you how proud she is, how proud everyone is. Up. Feel bad when you find out your roommate is head minute caller for Re-Orgy week, but since she's in the hospital, you'll have to do it. Down.

The day room was in the basement of the barracks, a room with a big television, thirty vinyl burnt orange chairs and three couches, and a pool table. Upperclassmen had day room privileges, but we plebes were only invited in for meetings. Captain DiBella, West Point class of 1969, was the first Army officer I ever met in uniform, in an official capacity. There was a tactical officer assigned to our Beast company, but I'd never met him and Captain Mulligan didn't really count (He had a golf shirt on and gave me ice cream.) Captain DiBella wore a Class A uniform, green jacket loaded with medals; he was polished and professional and may have just stepped off a recruiting poster. Did I say really good looking? After he introduced himself to us as the officer responsible for our health and welfare, he asked us to introduce ourselves to each other. We were a strange lot.

For someone like me, born and brought up on the same street my whole life, where everyone except the Smiths were Catholic and everyone except the DelVecchios were Irish, I felt like I'd been tossed into a National Geographic magazine. There were six females, including me. There were three black males. I'd never spoken to a black person in my life. There were some real geeks, who spoke only in multi-syllables with concerned, wrinkled foreheads and calculators attached to their belt loops. There were a few country folk, who talked like they'd lived next door to the Clampetts and had just come to the "big city" with Uncle Jed. And, slouched by the door, ready for a quick exit, there were the wild ones, the ones whose eyes gleamed; they were primed for adventure.

We were from all over: the Bronx, Alaska, Nevada and Florida. Dollar Bill, John T, Brian and Steve had been to the prep school; George had spent three years at New Mexico Military Institute; Bill had been to college for a year; most had come straight out of high school. We were the Cream of the Crop. Liz was there, the normal girl who had been on the bus on R-Day. Her roommate, Teesa, was blond and blue-eyed with fun written all over her. The other female room was the stuff bad sitcoms are made of. Felicia had frosted hair. My Aunt Alice had frosted hair, but she was fifty-five. Felicia also caked on gobs of make-up. I didn't get it when female cadets wore make-up. They may as well have just squeaked loudly, "I'm a FEMALE CADET!" Who wanted anyone to notice us? Most of us tried to hide our femininity, tried to fit in as regular sex-less cadets. Lori, Felicia's roommate, was her antithesis. She looked tough; nothing would or could bother her. She told us she was from Pittsburgh and played both softball and basketball and I figured she played them both hard. I left the day room wondering what kind of a melting pot I'd fallen into. I missed Robinson Avenue. I missed Kim, Sharon, Sean; I didn't make new friends well; I missed home.

Linda marched back from Lake Frederick with blisters the size of saucers on her feet. She had cellulitus and she couldn't walk. When I visited her in the hospital during a free twenty minute slot of time on Friday afternoon, I almost threw up when I saw her feet, the huge flaps of pale skin, the glossy red splotches of infected skin, but was I ever impressed. It was amazing that she made the entire march back with those feet. She'd refused to get on the sick call truck. All of us females felt the pressure of being able to hang, but she had the added pressure of being the daughter of the commander. She refused to give either her sex or her father a bad name.

She told me she felt bad she wouldn't be able to help me for our first S.A.M.I. in F-2.

"Hey, that's OK," I told her. "Don't worry about it."

She explained to me that her father had spent the past two years as the Regimental Tactical Officer (RTO) in charge of second regiment, under which F-2 fell. I thought she was making polite conversation. My response of "That's nice" forced her to explain to me, the numbskull, that her father had inspected many cadet rooms over the past two years and found many discrepancies and many cadets would now feel the urge to find many discrepancies in the room of his daughter. They would find this especially easy to do with Colonel West in Germany. He'd been transferred after Beast was over. Linda haunted me with "Don't forget to clean the baseboards!" as I left the hospital to get back in time for dinner formation and hours of scrubbing and folding and dusting.

That knock-knock always makes you jump. It was easier to face these inspections with someone waiting beside you. The company tactical officer, Captain DiBella, and the company commander, Cadet Kelly, walked in my room. I'd never been inspected by an officer before, and I reacted by freezing in place. I inhaled. Captain DiBella smiled. I wasn't used to inspectors smiling. I just kept inhaling. He really was good looking. He glanced around the room, opened the medicine cabinet, almost casually, asked me if I'd seen Linda in the hospital. *Hey, move things around! I dusted those bookshelves by the light of the moon since I had to have my lights out at Taps! I shined those shoes by flashlight!* He walked over to my closet and took one of my class shirts out, holding it by the hanger. They were short-sleeved dark gray button down shirts with a collar, ironed neatly by the laundry man. He held it up and showed Cadet Kelly, grinning, and said, "This would fit my eight year old son!" The entourage smiled slightly. I was still inhaling. He told me the room looked great and keep up the good work. I exhaled. The self-esteem took a little ride UP but I knew it would be short-lived. Such was the nature of this place.

✦ ✦ ✦ ✦

The afternoon after the S.A.M.I. was my second visit with my parents and the first time I'd seen Kim and Sharon since the spiked watermelon going away bash. Two things happened on that Saturday: Linda became an O'Sullivan; I learned Sean was seeing other girls.

I knew my parents would love Linda and they did. We visited her in the hospital and she was in their will the minute they saw her feet. I did not figure Sean would have another girlfriend so soon. I did not figure that he'd start going out with someone else without talking to me first, without talking about us breaking up, maybe seeing other people. I didn't think that after going out for three years together, he'd just dump me without some warning.

I was standing in my white over grey uniform, mailman hat and nun shoes, with Kim and Sharon, at the library corner, waiting for my parents to pick us up in the Dodge Colt and take us down by the river for chicken wings and chips and Kim was antsy. I knew something was up. She kept asking me about Sean and were we still going out, and I'd known Kim since before kindergarten. All the signs were there. She had gossip. I got it out of her in seconds. With Kim, it doesn't take much. Last Friday night, late, she'd seen Sean with Kathy Hyatt at McDonald's and yes, they looked pretty tight.

That fiddler's elbow, up and down. Up: My parents and Kim and Sharon were visiting; my mother brought me Half-Moons from DiMarino's bakery; my roommate was great; I had a good S.A.M.I. Down: My boyfriend dumped me. Down. Way down. Way, way down. Rock bottom. This wasn't a "cadet" down. This down had nothing to do with inspection arms or shooting sharpshooter. This down had everything to do with me, the person; me, the girl.

When he'd come up during Beast with my parents, it was weird. But we'd kept writing letters, glossing over life and acting like we could still go out even though the next time I'd see him would be Christmas. I'd been gone less than two months and he was going out with someone else and he didn't even tell me and my insides were torn up, hurt, and crying. But I'd mastered keeping that crying inside. One thing I'd learned in Beast was how to smile like my mother. I could be tired, sweaty, hot and my self-esteem at the depths of a bottomless swamp, but I was Little Miss Positive, making the most of being a female, a small, wimpy female, in a male institution. So my reaction to Sean's dumping me was what I'd learned in Beast: Smile and drive on. The other part of my reaction was probably not Beast related, just the hurt, burned Irish female in me: Never say a word to him again.

It's the first word in the West Point motto, followed only by Honor and Country, and they probably put it first for a reason. It *had* to be important. Duty. Every cadet has duties and the plebe duties were posted on the bulletin board across from the orderly room every Sunday night for the next week: mail carriers, laundry carriers, minute callers. One lucky plebe won the title of "Head"; this poor soul was responsible for the other six plebes who fall under his command. With Linda in the hospital during re-orgy, by default, I won her head minute caller duties. Minute callers basically just stand in the hallway getting yelled at or waiting to get yelled at. At attention, standing like dingbats under the clocks in the hallways, ten minutes before each formation, eyes straight ahead, shooting ducks for upperclassmen to criticize them for not having a good dress off, not knowing how many lights are in Cullum Hall, or for just breathing.

"Sir, there are ten minutes before assembly for breakfast formation. The uniform is as for class. For breakfast we are having pancakes, orange juice, assorted jellies and jams, assorted cereals. Ten minutes, Sir!"

There was a memorized blurb the minute callers sang out in unison, and then, within five seconds, no less than five upperclassmen appeared, like magic. Two were fully dressed, ready for formation, excited about spending the next eight minutes hazing their minute caller. *When did they get up? At dawn?* One would have his shoes off and have a cotton ball and shoe in his hand, shining it in his stocking feet as he asked me to start "The Days", another blurb we spit out, citing the exact number of days until significant cadet events, including Army-Navy, Christmas, and Graduation. The other two would have their shirttails outside their pants and just wander out to check out who this new plebe was under "their" clock. Sometimes, one of them hadn't zipped their fly yet. I wasn't sure if they knew. Maybe they just wanted to save the zip, figuring why bother now if I'm still going to pee before formation. Or maybe they knew and wanted me to gaze down and check out their package. I never gazed down there. Oh, please, Grow UP, I felt like saying.

"Where're you from, O'Sullivan?"

"Sir, may I make a statement."

"That's why I asked, O'Sullivan. Make your statement."

Playing the four answer game drove them crazy. I loved it. "Sir, I'm from Braintree, Massachusetts." Not one of them ever noted that my hometown was the birthplace of the father of West Point, Sylvanus Thayer. Honestly, they should have spent more time studying the history of their school.

"Do you think MAYBE my mother's third cousin Ernie is from Massachusetts, O'Sullivan?"

I keep quiet; I think *Thank God my great state can't claim you, you loser.*

"Look at the size of those feet! My baby brother in third grade has feet bigger than those, O'Sullivan! What do you say to that?"

"No excuse, Sir."

"You call that a dress-off, O'Sullivan?"

"No excuse, Sir."

"You're right NO EXCUSE! You'd better NEVER stand outside MY room and MY clock with a dress-off that looks so shabby! Get that, O'Sullivan?"

"Yes, Sir." *What a jerk. Did his family even like him?*

Upperclassmen at West Point were like Mrs. Flaherty. She always referred to her husband as "My John." My John is working on the car, My John is sick today. But Mrs. Flaherty just used the possessive for her John. These upperclassmen owned anything in their sight. My clock, My hallway, My company area, MY great state of Wisconsin, and even, You're breathing MY air. I figured it was a power trip, until I found myself doing it a few years later. It truly was an acquired habit.

"Do you think maybe" was another favorite. A typical statement from a young man who scored over 1300 on his SATs, was a member of the National Honor Society and delegate to Boys' State might be, "Do you think maybe I'm wondering WHAT you're doing in MY hallway with NO dress-off?"

It didn't happen to me during Re-orgy week, but it was a few weeks later when I was calling minutes and it was raining outside. The uniform, as stated in the blue book of cadet regulations, was as for class, under raincoats, wearing overshoes. We had rubber overshoes that fit snugly over our shoes, though no one liked to wear them - they messed up the shine. I hadn't worn them since kindergarten, when mine were red, and we hadn't called them overshoes. They were rubbers.

Understand that when I left home for West Point, the amount of knowledge I had about sex could squeeze into a small pea, those petite ones. My mother never told me anything. She claimed, exasperated and stuttering once when I asked her, that she had a book somewhere, but the book never materialized. I really don't think *she* knew. Sharon found out from Theresa McDonough and she relayed to me, but by the time I got the birds and the bees, it was a watered-down version. I wasn't allowed to watch "Love American Style," a TV show in the '70s, because it was "fresh." Seriously. When I heard the word Rubber, I thought *only* of the things you put on your feet when it rained. Not another thing came to mind.

So there I stood. "Sir, there are ten minutes until assembly for breakfast formation. The uniform is As for class, under raincoats, wearing rubbers. For breakfast we are having…"

Didn't have to finish. Couldn't even say Scrambled Eggs because there were eight upperclassmen, some still in their gym shorts, two in their bathrobes, all in my face.

"O'SULLIVAN! What did you say?!?"

Let's see. What did I say. It's still raining, isn't it?

"O'SULLIVAN! What did you say the uniform was?"

What are these guys? Morons? I can hear that rain! Isn't that rain, I hear? What's the big deal about wearing raincoats?

"Sir, may I make a statement?" Oh, great, here's Phillips, the jerk. Just what I need is one more jerk and not this one.

"What's Darla calling out here?"

Phillips was a firstie, second only to Disher in the Jerky Firsties category. He had nicknames for Linda and me. We couldn't stand him. He called me "Little Darla", from the Little Rascals in an unprofessional, repulsive way. He hazed Linda mercilessly, forcing her to stand outside his room after taps reciting knowledge, while he ranted and raved about her father, who had tried to kick him out but had been unsuccessful. He was creepy and mean-spirited and I hated when he called me Darla. But I never did anything about it.

"Tell us the uniform, O'Sullivan!"

"Sir, the uniform is as for class, under raincoats, wearing rubbers."

More hysterical laughter. I still don't see the humor.

"RUBBERS??? O'SULLIVAN??? RUBBERS????"

"Sir, may I make a statement?"

More of them are in the hallway, Some guys are yelling down the hall, "Hey, O'Sullivan says to wear our rubbers to formation!"

"Make your statement, O'Sullivan."

Like a mother explaining to her five year old, I said, "Sir, it's raining outside."

They finally fade away. Yelling and laughter down both sides of the hall. I see Cadet Damsel walking towards me. He gets close enough to say something without everyone hearing him.

"Cadet O'Sullivan," he says, in that quiet way. "The blue book says overshoes. Don't call them rubbers. Call them overshoes."

"Yes, Sir," I respond dutifully. What was all that about, I wonder.

I had a bit to learn.

✢ ✢ ✢

"...but most of all respect thyself."

—Pythagorean Precept

Certain plebes had a bull's eye on the front of their shirt. I'm not sure why. They were labeled as "tie-ups" (someone who never gets anything right). Some plebes didn't handle the harassment well and "spazzed" (messed up). Others had a look that an upperclassman didn't like. On the other hand, some plebes seemed impervious to the upperclassmen and unknowingly deflected the harassment onto their roommate or the poor guy sitting next to them at the table. I didn't have a bull's eye on my shirt. I think they felt bad for me. I was just a pathetic creature and I just tried so hard. Linda didn't have a bull's eye either, but she did have a few upperclassmen who very immaturely took out their feelings towards her father, on her.

It was her birthday. October 13, 1978. She was nineteen years old, her family was in Germany, and Cadet Disher was her table commandant. She massacred the dessert, he told her. She needed some "A.I.", additional instruction. Swing by his room after dinner for correction. She did. She came back to our room in tears. He'd told her to stand at attention in front of his wardrobe for over ten minutes, hazing her like there was no tomorrow. *That* she could take. What she could *not* take was the uniform he chose to haze her in. His underwear.

But we never did anything about it.

I could only hope I'd do better in academics. I'd been dumped by my boyfriend and every day was a bad hair day and I didn't have a military bone in my body and I proved that daily throughout the summer, and, yes, this *was* a military academy, and, *hello*, should I be concerned? I didn't think about it; I just hoped I could redeem myself during the academic year.

I *had* to do better in academics. I was more comfortable with a calculus book than a pugil stick. I assumed my odds of failing a class were less than those of falling out of a road march. I liked doing homework. I liked taking notes. I was on the math team in high school.

Every class was two tons harder than I thought they would be. Even without having to actually go to the class, pay attention, stay awake, and do the homework, life was hard. We were up by 6:00 a.m. to shower and get dressed, get our rooms ready for the morning inspection (called A.M.I. but, for some reason, not "Ammy"), stand in breakfast formation, eat breakfast like a plebe, ping back to our rooms, grab our books and ping, faster than the speed of light, at attention, to our first class. Linda and I walked together, no talking, to Thayer Hall for calculus or Bartlett Hall for chemistry, then separated inside the door, to find our classrooms. I dreaded being Section Marcher, the cadet responsible for accountability in the classroom. I preferred the back row, but in History, where no Ns or O'Briens were around (we were placed in most classes by alphabetical order), I was the Section Marcher. Every morning, after counting heads, I called the room to attention and stated to Captain Harper, "Sir, Cadet O'Sullivan reports. All cadets are present." Captain Harper kidded around, updated us on the Red Sox and Bruins. He was an ROTC grad from Providence and sometimes, if the sun was shining, he even moved our class outside, down by the river. Not all P's (short for professor. All the teachers were referred to as "P's") were so kind.

Math Ps were reputedly the worst, but I didn't get what the big hoopla was all about. Archbishop Williams had prepared us well. None of the Math Ps in Thayer Hall came came close to the five-foot-tall dynamo that Jimmy, Mike, Patty and I had for three years in high school. Sister Patricia Ann drilled more than integrals in our heads. She taught us how to take notes, how to behave, how to study. At West Point, the scary aspect of math was "taking boards," working a problem on the board, then reciting and explaining it while enduring the probing questions of the P. We'd done this daily in Sister Patricia Ann's class, and I can still see her hovering over Jimmy Mac's board work, demanding, "Mister McConville, how did you come up with THAT?" I hated math in high school, and after a week in Calculus at West Point, I realized what a great teacher she was.

In my grammar school, corporal punishment was as much a part of the routine as recess. We met it early on in first grade when Joey Shaughnessy got his report card and Sister Katrina yanked him into the inner office, closed the door and paddled his little bottom. She put the microphone nearby and turned the loud speaker on. The whole school cringed as he wailed. In high school, corporal punishment wasn't necessary. We wailed without the paddle. Bloody, our French teacher, who didn't get that nickname for being a push-over, had the ability to put a student (or more) in tears on demand, without ever raising her voice. They may not have worn Ranger tabs, but the nuns who I knew growing up, were tough cookies.

The discipline was no big deal, but the academics just bowled me over. Before West Point, I'd been devastated by one C in 5th grade and I'd received some B's over the years, but I'd figured out how to get mostly A's and found that I really liked them. *That was Then, this is Now.*

Engineering Fundamentals was harder than using directions written in Chinese to put a rocket ship together. Do-loops and a strange animal called Fortran made absolutely no sense at all. *Terrain Analysis and Evaluation* made me wish I'd learned how to read a map growing up, instead of stopping at Citgo stations and asking for directions. And then there was *Military Science*, a subject like nothing I'd ever seen before in my life. I dealt with confusion by memorizing. I grew to love acronyms because they made the memorization easier: OCOKA (Observation, Cover and Concealment, Obstacles, Key Terrain, Avenues of Approach) was how you determined your axis of attack and MOSSMOUSE (Mass, Objective, Surprise, Security, Maneuver, Offensive, Unity of Command, Simplicity and Economy of Force) were the Principles of War. Don't ask me how to apply them, but I could rattle them off with the future Great War strategists, who always sat beside me in class and made me feel like Gilligan, lost on an island I had no business being on.

English class sucked the final breaths of air out of my already deflated self-esteem. I thought I could write. I won the "Excellence in English" award in high school! Then I got my first paper back in plebe English, an essay on Tokyo Rose, and she bled in red pen corrections. I got a C. All through Beast, I never cried in front of anyone. I almost lost it in that English class in Mahan Hall when Major Privatsky handed back Tokyo Red Rose.

Academics couldn't give a compliment without attaching a big "But." Like my Nana, every Thanksgiving, saying to my mother, "Isn't this turkey delicious nutritious. But is it fresh?" (My mother soon learned to nod and smile and hide the yellow plastic wrap that said Butterball.)

We took a diagnostic test during Beast and they put me in Accelerated French. Thanks to years of Bloody beating Francais into my head with a brick, I got an A+. Two years of high school Spanish and that Boston accent, which everyone kept insisting that I owned, apparently did little for my French accent. My French P, a nice guy, told me, with some amusement, that I had the highest average in French, but the absolute worst pronunciation he had ever heard in his life. *But is it fresh?*

When I walked through the doors of the gymnasium at West Point, in my white t-shirt that said O'Sullivan, my black shorts, my white ankle socks and converse sneakers, I felt like I'd been blasted out of a cannon and landed with a thump on Uranus. My disciplined education may have prepared me well for the academic rigors of West Point, but it did zilch for me in the world of physical fitness.

"Do not attempt to do a thing unless
you are sure of yourself; but do not
relinquish it simply because someone
else is not sure of you."

—Stewart E. White

At my high school, in gym class, we put on our navy blue jumpers that snapped down the front and covered the navy blue bloomers beneath, then meandered up to the gym where we played twenty minutes of volleyball or kickball or some such unorganized leisure sport. The locker room was used for storage, which was fine, since no one ever sweated. No one came close to even waking up a sweat gland. I never ran a mile, never did sit-ups or push-ups. PE was Miss McLaughlin trying to organize an unruly group of girls in navy bloomers, with half of the class sitting in the bleachers watching because they had their periods, or said they did anyway.

So, I was as worried about PE as I'd been about the road marches. Everyone back home, *everyone*, predicted that physical fitness would be my exit cue. I figured that surviving the summer had been just lucky; that the worst was yet to come; that it would come in the form of PE class at Arvin Gymnasium.

Male plebes took boxing and wrestling. They replaced these classes with Self-Defense I and II for the female plebes and this caused some animosity among the males who thought the females were "getting over", an expression for having an easy out. HA! Imagine this: You weigh ninety-five pounds soaking wet. You beat Lori Houlihan up in sixth grade, but since then, you haven't hurt a fly. You haven't had the slightest urge to hurt a fly and no one has ever had the slightest urge to hurt you. You actually take pride in being nice to people. eighteen years of non-violence that would make Mahatma Gandhi look like a ruffian and now you find yourself lying on your back on a matted floor in a wrestling room. Less than three feet away from you is Lori, the stud, who could kick most of your male classmates' skinny little asses. Dr. Peterson, the same lady from the "New Kid In Town" movie during Beast, is referred to as The Dragon Lady, not because she is a push-over. She blows her whistle and you scurry up and try to defend yourself, but before you're even off the ground, you have failed to successfully block a round-house kick and you've been hurled through the air across the room. Then you hear the Dragon Lady say, very matter-of-factly, "That was O'Sullivan! You can throw her farther than that!"

This was "getting over"?

If possible, swimming was even worse. I should have known it wouldn't be pretty when we had our first exposure to the Department with A Heart, the pet name for Department of Physical Education, during our swimming test, held in the gigantic indoor pool on a breezy, rainy day during Beast. My last bathing suit experience involved lying on the beach at Nantasket listening to "Someone's Gonna Take My Kodachrome Awaaaay" and reading Seventeen magazine.

The most awful part of it was wearing the female cadet issue bathing suit, officially the world's most ugly bathing suit, including a black and white suit with a skirt that my mother wore that had people all over it eating in cafes and smiling wide smiles, across her breasts and butt. The female cadet issued bathing suit was almost a slinky turtleneck, a black tank suit with a gold stripe down the sides, and the sizes were one size will fit all. The small was not intended for someone who had no breasts and, missing the very essential padding that all my two pieces must have, it hung off me in the breasts, screaming NO CHEST, NO SHAPE. I looked hideous. Not only that, but I'd never passed advanced beginners in third grade at Sunset Lake, and then, after that humiliating failure, had never taken another swimming lesson in my life. I was pretty certain I'd meet my maker in the bottom of the pool in Arvin Gymnasium. And when I did meet Him, I'd be looking pretty bad in that suit.

My jaw dropped and hit my knees when I saw the guys lining the pool walls wearing their tiny black Speedos. Except for an occasional Canadian tourist, no one wore Speedos in Massachusetts. Until that swim test in Beast, I'd never seen a guy wear anything but dungaree shorts to swim in. It was hard to not smile when I saw, standing shivering by the side of the pool, fifty of my classmates, nervous and pasty, wearing what we called at home "grape smugglers."

I was placed in Advanced Beginners, known as Advanced Rocks, one step above the pure Rocks, the kids from Iowa who had never seen water before in their life in anyplace but the kitchen sink. The military swim portion almost ended my short life, but, fortunately, I had my priorities straight. Though I did hope to excel, my drive to live was greater. I was doing the required swim down a lane, wearing my fatigues and boots, carrying an M-16, when, after a few feet, I came to the realization that I was indeed going to drown. After but a moment of hesitation, I did some quick decision-making and dropped the M-16, watching it sink to the bottom as I slowly floated back up to the top. I looked anxiously over at the instructor, who always positioned himself by the hook on the wall when I was in the water, and he said to me, simply, with patience, "Do it again." He seemed to feel my pain.

I went back and did it again. Same deal. I feel myself being pulled down; I feel the water rising slowly all around me. This time I flail and kick and paddle, but gravity is still winning. I drop the weapon again. The instructor walks over to the edge of the pool and kneels down beside me, waiting for me to get some air and stop coughing up chlorine. He's clearly angry, but there's another look on his face. Worry? Concern? I know this Department is known for its P's being ruthless ogres, but they are all nice to me. I think they feel bad for me. He asks, "What happened?" I pause. I look like a drowned rat with big frightened eyes; I look up at him, and humbly admit, "Sir, it was either me or my weapon…"

I finally swim the entire lane, jump off the ten-meter platform in my fatigues, a requirement to pass the class, and put the world's ugliest bathing suit away until the next summer, when it would only hang off me even more.

Mrs. Herrick's lessons behind the K of C Hall paid off in gymnastics and I finally could do something: the cartwheels and handstands. I'd never been on a horizontal ladder or climbed a rope before in my life. Never. But with much practice, both the ladder and rope were do-able. They were essentials as they were both part of the Indoor Obstacle Course, one of the three physical fitness tests held by DPE throughout the academic year for grade. These tests were not optional. These tests were called "Big Sucks."

The Indoor Obstacle Course was somewhere between three to six minutes of agony and there was no doubt in my mind that I would fail it. Set up in the oldest, mustiest, dirtiest, dustiest part of the gym, it involves crawling under wire, climbing up onto a wooden shelf, crossing parallel bars, vaulting the pommel horse, jumping over a wall, crossing the horizontal ladder, climbing the ten foot high rope, jumping through tires like a football player, and running three laps carrying a ten pound medicine ball. The IOC was one of those things that made you say, "Wouldn't it be nice to have some upper body strength today!"

The shelf is infamous for us short female cadets with miniscule biceps and zero pecs, and the few short male cadets who weren't gymnasts or wrestlers. Gymnasts and wrestlers whiz through the course, jumping onto the six-foot high shelf like a frog hopping onto a lily pad. The concept is that with a running start, the cadet approaches the shelf, jumps up, grabs the shelf by the ledge that runs along the inside top of the shelf, swings the leg and then the entire body onto the shelf, and continues onto the next obstacle. The reality for me was very different than the concept. The reality was that I ran full speed toward the shelf, stopped, jumped, grabbed onto the ledge, hung and started swinging my legs furiously, like the cartoon Road Runner when he's mid-air after falling off that cliff. The pendulum motion must have made me feel like I was doing something; I was really going nowhere fast. After a few seconds of solid effort, I dropped and, dejected, head hung low, walked over to the Ladder For Motor Retards, specifically put in place for those with twig-like arms who could not negotiate the shelf. Taking a penalty on my time, but even worse, taking a serious blow to the self-esteem, I climbed the ladder, humiliating every bone in my body, and continued the rest of the course, figuring it couldn't get any worse, though it usually did. Every time I took the IOC, the last event for me was the race to the wastepaper basket to dry heave.

The first DPE test was the two mile run course down along the river by the sewerage plant. The reeking odors, the cadets vomiting along the side of the course, the long, steep walk back up to the barracks were all integral parts of the two-mile run. I was doomed. Not only had I never run a race for time before in my life, but this race was in combat boots. In those days, we wore boots for our physical fitness runs. Linda, who had run track in high school, offered to pace me and we ran together, finishing in less than fifteen minutes. Immediately after the run, we dressed for lunch formation and got the third degree from the upperclassmen on our times. Linda and I, red faced and sore, were surprised by the attention we received. They smiled. They were proud of "their female cadets." Still a long way from feeling accepted, the re-action wasn't the usual toleration that we felt. It was kind of nice.

The Army Physical Fitness Test (called the APFT) of the seventies went out with the combat boots. It was a combination test: the run, dodge and jump, the broad jump, sit-ups, the inverted crawl, and the two-mile run. The run, dodge and jump was almost fun. You ran around some hurdles, politely marked with arrows telling you which way to run, jumped over a moat, and ran around some more hurdles. The inverted crawl, more commonly known as the "perverted crawl," was the great equalizer. Even the hunkiest of men looked clumsy and goofy doing a crab walk with arms moving faster than legs and bodies trying to catch up, often landing with a thud on their back-sides. The scores from all events were compiled to give one composite score, which meant disaster could be saved by cranking out some sit-ups or run-ning well. This test allowed for second chances, unlike the Indoor Obstacle Course, where that blasted shelf could lead in mere seconds to mediocrity at best, failure more probable.

"Upon the fields of friendly strife
are sown the seeds that upon
other fields, on other days,
will bear the fruit of victory."

—General Douglas MacArthur

All cadets are athletes; they breathed, they ate, they were athletes. MacArthur was big on it and he ruled the block. If not involved in an intercollegiate sport, called a corps-squad sport, cadets participated in intramural or club sports. There were two good things about rabble-rousing. First, we got out of parades. Corps squad and Club squad didn't have to carry that M-14 on parade days; they were authorized to be practicing their sport. The second good thing about rabble-rousing was that I couldn't do anything else. Every sport under the sun is offered at West Point, from crew to water polo to orienteering to squash, but due to complete and total lack of competence and coordination, I recognized my inability to participate in any of them. Fortunately, I could yell, climb to the top of pyramids and be thrown in the air by male cadets.

I thought it would be cool. I honestly didn't think I was vain, but I admit I would have liked to have been cool. High school cheerleaders were cool so I assumed college cheerleaders were even cooler. At this time in West Point's history, this was not the case. I'm not sure why. Maybe it was looks. I should have taken a closer look in the mirror, though I'm glad I didn't; who needed *that*? The normal college cheerleader, from say Boston College or Notre Dame, wore cute, teeny, tight uniforms that hung somewhere about mid-buttocks, snazzy bleach-white sneakers, had long wavy hair, usually blond, and frequented a tanning booth prior to showing her eight foot long legs. The West Point cheerleader, circa 1977-1978 wore big gold sweaters, gold wool skirts, hideous gold pumas, had their hair shaved by Big Ed with one single blade, and hadn't seen the sun in anything but fatigues and a steel pot for three months. Forget looking hot; I wasn't even luke-warm.

Rabble-rousers in general took a hit in popularity. It was purely a matter of testosterone. The corps of cadets, about 4,000 males, ages eighteen to twenty-two, generally prefer head butting to chess. It would follow that they would label football players as macho, rabble-rousers as wimps. Cadets dealt with anyone they thought lesser of in very mature ways, like throwing milk cartons out the window at them. I thought this was all in the spirit of things until the night I was crossing the area after an impromptu spirit rally, wearing my bright gold sweater, and took a tomato to the head. I realized that this was not the quickest route to homecoming court, though homecoming court was not an option anyway. That was only for civilian girls. The first two years I was at West Point, the corps voted for women whose glossies, tastefully done, of course, were hung in the hallways by their proud boyfriends. No pictures of anyone in dress grey were up there.

Though the term "rabble rouser" elicited a snicker from the corps, individually, the male rabble-rousers were well liked. What a great group of guys. Their friendship salvaged my self-esteem. In corps squad sports, the plebes are "recognized", called by their first name, by their teammates. I "sir'd" the upperclass rabble-rousers to death. I was a worrier and a rule follower, and didn't want to come close to the possibility of a romantic thing. Either thanks to Big Ed or their professionalism, no one ever tried to develop any sort of romantic relationship with me. They were like big brothers looking out for me, trying to get me to lighten up.

> **"Most people are about as happy as**
> **they make their minds up to be."**
>
> **—Abraham Lincoln**

Not so with the female rabble-rousers, all yearlings, all members of the first class with women, the Class of 1980. Danna, the cadet Patty and I had met the previous spring and the one who met me and Janet in the woods at Lake Frederick, was friendly and concerned; and, Carol and Kathy were kind, but the others maintained a distance that offended and, regrettably, resulted in my stereotyping the women members of the Class of 1980. Desperate for mentoring by a female, my first disappointing experiences with them in rabble-rousing, led me to stereotype them in a negative way.

I knew there were exceptions. The yearling women rabble-rousers didn't haze us. They just ignored us. If they didn't want to recognize us, I could live with that. What baffled me was their lack of understanding and concern. There seemed to be an underlying sentiment that said, "We had it harder." They seemed to want to sing along with Helen Reddy, "I am Woman, Hear me Roar."

Example: Liz was pinging out of the mess hall after breakfast, racing to get back to the barracks, up the five flights of stairs, grab her books and get to class, when she heard "Halt, Miss!" It was a female yearling who stopped her because she claimed Liz's hips were swaying as she walked. The woman made Liz practice walking back and forth in the middle of the area, made her try to keep her hips stationary as her legs moved, while passing cadets stopped to watch the spectacle. Even if Liz had sashayed like a pendulum, a good leader, one whose shoulders were not chipped to pieces, would have taken her aside and talked to her, would have treated her the way she herself would have liked to have been treated. This was unfortunately typical of the treatment of the women by the women.

Patty and I wondered if along with the bitterness and anger that these women developed during their developed during their very difficult, ground-breaking plebe year, there was just some plain old female jealousy involved. Patty was tall and thin. Most of the other plebe women were as small as I was. The male rabble-rousers preferred to toss us up in the air and we wondered if the yearlings didn't like sharing the attention of being THE women at West Point, with, not only other women, but with smaller women.

Whatever the rationale behind their attitude, I developed my own. Before the first football game, I began to stereotype the women in the Class of 1980 as bitter, angry feminists with a serious chip on their shoulder. Bitterness swept humor under the rug, swept it hard. It was so far under that rug, it probably didn't come out again for years. I needed humor and was convinced it was absolutely necessary to survive West Point. I didn't endure what they endured, but I knew I didn't want to become what I saw they had become. My attitude toward these trail-blazers was a shame; both of our classes needed support, not alienation.

There were pro's and con's to wearing those gold pumas. The biggest advantage was being able to get away from West Point. Plebes couldn't leave West Point until Christmas, so belonging to a team or club that took you out the gate was a huge deal. Thanks to rabble rousing, I was going to go to the Boston College football game and I'd be able to spend the night at home in my old bed, for the first time in almost four months. My parents and their friends, the card club in force, had tickets and coolers ready for the game. I'd drive home with them after the game and be back on Sunday to catch the bus back to West Point with the other cadets who were on this "trip section." I was counting down the days.

The weekend before the game, my right foot began to ache. It slowly started to swell, growing and hurting more by the hour. By Tuesday, I couldn't get my foot in my shoe, but Linda wore the same size five shoes, only in a wider width, and we had been issued two pairs of shoes. I put my shoe on my left foot and her shoe on my right foot, and limped slightly down to formation. It was 6:30 a.m. in October in New York and dark enough where no one would notice my two different shoes, I thought.

My foot was painful and grossly swollen, but I never thought about going to a doctor. During Beast, the upperclassmen told us, loudly and often, that female cadets went on sick call more than male cadets; female cadets were trying to "get over." I hadn't gone on sick call yet and unless my shin bone jutted out of my skin or buckets of blood oozed from an orifice, I didn't plan on going anytime soon.

The limp gave me away. It hurt too much to not limp. One of the upperclassmen saw me, came over, and innocently asked, "O'Sullivan, you limping?"

"Sir, may I make a statement?"

"Yeah, O'Sullivan. It looked like you were limping."

"Yes, Sir."

He was looking at my feet. I had no trouble remaining stoic in the face of hazing, but if an upperclassman showed me any care or understanding, for some reason, I became more emotional. So, when this cadet asked me, with obvious concern,

"Do you have two different shoes on?"

I replied, "Yes, Sir" in a weak, kind of giving up way.

He asked gently, "Why?"

My voice quivered as I said, resignedly, "Sir, one of my feet keeps getting fatter and I don't know why."

He made me go immediately to sick call. They told me I had cellulitis. Bad. It had spread to my lymph nodes. They hooked me up to an IV and admitted me. They told me I'd be there for at least a week. I shouldn't have waited so long, they scolded.

Two funny things happened in the hospital. First, they put me in a crib. I was eighteen years old and in a crib. There were no available beds. The hospital was still in the cadet area in these days, an old stone monster with crooked hallways and giant ceilings, and not enough space so I lay in an iron, white, railed crib. Did my life at West Point bring me from one embarrassing moment to the next or what?

Second, I had a roommate who was a very strange bird. I looked at her, listened to her and thanked God for Linda. This girl should have been in a hospital that had padded cells. She was fruitier than a fruitcake. Thank goodness for small favors, she was thrown out on an honor code violation within the year.

My immediate concern, other than people seeing me in a crib, was that I would not be able to go to the Boston College game. I was devastated. Every time the doctor came in, I begged and pleaded. I hadn't called my parents because I didn't want them to worry and I really didn't know what was going to happen to my big B.C. weekend. I only called home on Sunday afternoons, collect, anyway, so I didn't think they would miss me.

They did. Captain DiBella visited me in the hospital and told me he had spoken to my parents. His wife also came to visit me, bringing me normal magazines, and just being motherly and friendly, concerned and worried. I thought, *She had to get a babysitter to come visit me. How nice of her.* She couldn't have realized that by visiting that little female cadet, she'd set the standard for a future Army wife.

My parents, it seems, had called the barracks and been told by some dumb yearling that I was in the hospital, and this put them right over the edge, naturally. The Tac found out, called them, and assured them I'd be all right. I never asked if he had spoken to the doctor, but I was released the afternoon before the game and was allowed to go on the trip section. It was sleeting, misty and bitter when the bus pulled into Alumni Stadium at Boston College. I was on crutches. My hair had been shredded by Big Ed. I'd lost weight. It could probably be said that I wasn't looking my best. My parents were mortified. They told me, the first time of many times, that I did not have to stay at West Point, that I was always welcome to come home.

> "My interest is in the future because I am
> going to spend the rest of my life there."
>
> —Charles F. Kettering

It had been a month and a half since Kim had told me about seeing Sean with another girl. I'd compartmentalized that bit of information in a back room of my brain, locked the door and tossed the key. Never said anything to my parents. Never said anything to Sean. We'd been writing letters to each other, glossing over life, not going into anything too real. I never asked him about Kathy Hyatt. I never wrote to him about Bob, a classmate I sort of liked; he never wrote about girls. I never asked; he never asked. We were heterosexual pre-cursors of the "Don't Ask; Don't Tell" philosophy. My parents, thoughtful and clueless, bought tickets for Kim, Sharon, and Sean to go to the game. I acted like a twelve year old and ignored him the whole game. After the game, we said good-bye, like he'd been my third cousin whom I'd seen at family reunions every fifth year. It was a forever kind of good bye, a sad way, the wrong way, to leave someone who'd been a best friend for three years.

> "Away, away, away we go / What care we for any foe?
> Up and down the field we go / Just to beat the Navy.
> A-R-M-Y! T-E-A-M!"
>
> —Old Corps Cheer

The first Saturday in December was The Day.

"Sir, there are three and a butt days until Army beats the Hell out of Navy at John Fitzgerald Kennedy Memorial Stadium in Philadelphia, Pennsylvania in football, SIR!" It was part of our required knowledge and we'd been rattling it off, counting down the days, since R-Day. I was excited because I could go to Philly early for the game (any time away from West Point is good time) and I was going to cheer on the sidelines of this huge stadium. Very high speed for me; I'd come a long way from Ridge Ice Skating Arena.

Army-Navy 1977 was the coldest I've ever been in my life and that includes a case of frost-bite I got years later in the Army in the field in Korea in January with no stove. In Korea, I wasn't wearing a rabble-rouser outfit. In our beige tights, skirts, and gold sneakers, we froze our hands, toes and butts off on that miserably, windy day with temperatures hovering around zero. Now, as an old grad, I understand the importance of this game, and I'm ashamed to admit that during my first Army-Navy as a cadet, I could have cared less if they won or lost. I only wanted it to over; I only wanted to be warm. Army actually won which now, as an old grad, I realize is a bigger deal than the Pope getting married. Rumor had it before the game, that if Army won, the plebes would be able to fall out in the mess hall for the rest of the year. That meant eat regular, big bites, gaze around, like a real person. It never happened. Rumors at West Point were usually wishful thinking, as accurate as the National Enquirer, as fast-spreading as a middle-aged waistline.

We all stayed in Philadelphia, where parties were rampant and we got to wear civilian clothes. I spent the night wandering our hotel with Patty, looking for Bob. Bob was a hockey player from Milton, the town right next to Braintree back home. I'd had a crush on him since Beast. He'd been in Seventh Company, Hellfire and Brimstone, Sir and I'd made it a point to eat my Oreos near him every Wednesday night at chapel (There were limited ways a new cadet can actually flirt with another new cadet and this was one of them.) We had become friends, sometimes a little bit more, but nothing too exciting. We danced at Eisenhower Hall on Saturday nights in that white over grey uniform—how exciting is that?

I finally found Bob after the game and then I spent the night wondering if we were going out. This was a sad pattern that most heterosexual female cadets fell into during their cadet careers. I wanted a boyfriend and I wanted it to be Bob. I was practical: Christmas was around the corner and wouldn't it be nice to have a boyfriend who lived in the next town. Wouldn't it be nice for him to see me in regular clothes and do regular things like go to the movies or the mall. It would have been nice, but winning the lottery would have been nice, too. It wasn't going to happen. Three words put a Cease-fire

Gail leading a cheer at an Army football game

on my plans: Girlfriend Back Home. Girlfriend Back Home was a real kick in the gut. First, there is a huge implication that this Girlfriend Back Home is Normal and you, the CADET, are not. We got used to it, but it was never easy to hear or stomach.

Christmas leave finally came. I slept the entire ride home. Back in Braintree, I missed Sean. I was back in the past, feeling like my old self, wearing my old clothes, in my old house. I wanted to be a part of the past again, just for the two weeks I'd be in it, but the way I'd acted at the B.C. game made that impossible. It was still so relaxing being home, in my house, in my bed, and not in the barracks. I ran miles through the streets of Braintree, bundled up in sweats and mittens, hoping Sean would see me, but I didn't call him. I was stubborn and hurt. He had a life; I didn't.

It was weird seeing my high school friends. We were living in two different worlds and they would never understand what I had done, what I was going though. We had all been fairly nerd-like in high school, but I had left and gone into an even more conservative world and they hadn't. They were partying and enjoying college life. I was studying and saluting telephone repairmen in the area. We got together for the first time to do our annual Christmas gift exchange. Sharon and I had seen each other, had kept in touch with letters, and we'd never change. There was a bond with her and Kim that would survive this West Point experience, but I wasn't so sure about the other girls in our group. When two of them gave me their Christmas gift, "The History of Tanks" (they'd chipped in and they were absolutely serious), I knew I was in trouble. Sometimes friendships are just paused for a few years until you're both in the same place again.

The bummers of Christmas leave plebe year: Getting that book on tanks, finding out my mother gave Aunt Joan all my prom dresses because "you'll never wear those pretty dresses again," and not having Sean around. The plusses: sleep, wearing civilian clothes all the time, sleep, eating all the devil dogs and fritos my mother had bought just for me, and more sleep. The biggest negative of Christmas leave though was the fact that it was finite. And it was over too fast.

seven

Gloom Period

"I haven't a clue as to how my story will end.
But that's all right. When you set out on a journey
and night covers the road, you don't conclude that the
road has vanished. And how else could we discover the stars?"

—Unknown

I was homeless.

I'd been sleeping since Connecticut and when I woke up, it was with a jump. My mind spun: *Where Am I!?!?* Then: *Damn!!!* I didn't swear so the *damn* part was a big deal.

That's when I realized I was homeless, after the *damn*. I thought, I want to go home again. But then the truths hit, bang, bang, bang, one after another.

Home to what?

My family doesn't know me anymore.

My friends are all different.

My boyfriend has a girlfriend who doesn't march to class in a uniform.

My closet is filled with my mother's summer clothes.

Nothing's the way it was;

I have no home!

"Honey," my father interrupted my internal mope session. "Your mother feels badly about you being gone on your birthday."

That was my father. My mother was next to him in the front seat but sometimes he acted as an interpreter for her. I don't know why.

"No big deal, Mom." I lied.

My Christmas vacation was over and my parents were driving me back to the United States Military Academy at West Point. It was January 3, 1978, two days before my birthday. I'd turn nineteen in a barracks room. I'd turn nineteen in a place no one wanted me to be.

I felt like a lead weight. I sank down into the cold red vinyl seat, weighed down by my depression, still and sad. My eyes watered as we drove through the granite gate, past the chunks of dirt encrusted snow that lined the sanded road. Half of plebe year was over; the hard part was behind us. But rational thought does nothing to alleviate that nauseous feeling that hits every cadet when driving through Thayer Gate after Christmas leave. It's like finding out that you didn't make the team, are too old for Santa, and have a terminal illness all at the same time.

The cloudless skies were grey; the sun was long gone. I held back tears. I still wanted my parents to think that I was tougher than I was. I didn't want them to think that I'd made a mistake in choosing to go to this place.

We pulled up and parked in front of Grant Barracks. My father got out of the car first; I dragged myself out after him and let him open the trunk and pull my suitcase out. He looked as bad as I felt. We weren't allowed to hug. No public displays of affection. My mother, smelling of hair spray and stale coffee, looked worse than my father. She tried to sneak a half-hug in; I shrugged her off, afraid of being seen and getting in trouble.

"Sorry," I mumbled. She looked hurt. I felt bad.

My father told me to hang in there. My mother told me she loved me and that I was Tough as Nails. She'd been calling me "Tough as Nails" since R-day and I was pretty sure she said it to make her think I really was.

I brought the suitcase up, hugging it to my chest with both hands, using it as a good excuse to not have to salute anyone. Then I walked away from my mother and father, eyes straight ahead, at attention, 180 steps per minute, toward my cadet room on the fifth floor of Central Barracks.

We'd sent our mattress covers to the laundry plant before we left for Christmas. Two bare mattresses, two bare beds and two dressers were stacked against the walls so the floors could be waxed when we were gone. My roommate wasn't back yet. I closed the door behind me and started to move the furniture. The room was cold; the heat blew puffs of quasi-warmth mocking the icy walls. I kept my ski jacket and gloves on. I dragged the dressers, desks and beds so they were a fist distance away from the walls, like the blue book said. Then I sat on the bare bed and put my head in my hands. I rubbed my eyes and tried not to cry. I tried to think of happy things. I came up with nothing.

I unpacked and waited for Linda. She'd flown to Germany to see her family for the first time since August. She looked as bad as I felt when she asked me, "How was your leave?"

"Great," I responded. "How was yours?"

"Great."

We both looked at each other and at our room. I saw tears welling up in her blue eyes and that was all I needed. My eyes watered and the tears spurted waterfalls flowing down my cheeks. We both sat on our beds and cried. We usually gave each other the "get tough" look; the "we can do this" gesture; the "this too shall pass" pep talk. On the day that plebes return to West Point after Christmas leave, these techniques are useless. You can be tough as nails and still need a good cry every once in awhile.

We all take beatings throughout life. At West Point, the "beatings," the challenges, are said to "develop character." Early on, plebes learn that to get up again, after having been beaten down, you need help. Linda and I would have cried each other through that first day back after Christmas leave. We would have survived that "beating" and added another gallon of character in the process. But we received some help, which not only boosted our morale, but taught us both a thing about mentorship and leadership.

We had our good cry, wiped our eyes and went back to work trying to get our room straight when we heard that familiar "Knock, Knock" at the door. We looked at each other with a mutual "Oh, No, I'm not ready for this" look.

"Come in, Sir," we said.

In walked Danna, the yearling from the company upstairs, holding two ice cream sundaes in her hand. She looked at us and in her casual, concerned way, said, "Hey! How's it going? Listen, this was the worst day of my life last year and I was thinking about you two and knowing you'd be pretty down, so thought I'd bring you some ice cream."

Almost every time I was beaten down, someone provided that concerned word, that kind act that could pick me up and jump-start me again. The fourth class system, by forcing us to be on the receiving end of the developing leadership styles of the upperclassmen, enabled us to see first hand which styles were most effective. The kindness approach worked for me; meanness only convinced me that the "leader" was, in West Point lingo, a Dick.

The Admissions catalog didn't mention the dismal, cold weather that accompanies the winter months along the Hudson River in New York. The gray skies that awaited us when we returned from Christmas leave stayed put, like a permanent attachment descending from the heavens and hooking onto the turrets on top of the Protestant Chapel. This was Gloom Period. Just when you think it's bad, it gets worse. We returned from Christmas leave to face not only this Greenland-like weather, but worse: our term-end examinations, the dreaded TEE's. These were exams that took three-four hours, in every subject, and for our class, they were held, for some heartless reason, after Christmas break. The only advantage of TEE's was that upperclassmen were too concerned about their own academic success to bother messing with the fourth class.

After my initial rough start in English, I got my act together, though I may have only looked good because so many classmates looked bad. I was surprised and dismayed to learn, though, that, after our TEEs were graded, they moved me to yearling English for second semester. English 201, Comparative Literature, should have been called "How To Take A Subject You've Always Liked and Learn to Hate It Overnight."

The instructor was a large, bald major, red faced, like he was perhaps menopausal. He must have assumed I was cocky (*like I had asked for this?*) and he took it upon himself to knock me down a couple of hundred pegs. He tore my papers apart. He single-handedly made me feel dumber than all of my first semester professors put together, which was really dumb. They make movies about people who are this dumb. I was the only plebe in this class of yearlings, commonly referred to as "yuks." "Yuks" is a good synonym; it reminds me of knuckleheads, coconuts, goofballs, dimwits, and that's what yearlings are, really. Major Whaley did not tell me to recognize the yearlings in my class, so I didn't, and I had to call them all "sir" in class discussions and conversations about our homework. Isn't that conducive to fun learning. English jumped quickly from my very short list of preferred subjects to my much longer list of subjects to be endured.

Two things other than the weather, which went from freezing to Arctic, changed after TEE's. I got new roommates and I didn't rabble-rouse. Every cadet switched roommates after the first semester, no preferences allowed, and I sadly left Linda to join Lori and Liz in a three-man—well, woman—room. These rooms were a bit larger than two men/women rooms; they had bunk beds and a single bed, still no flowered wallpaper. I went into the new room batting .500. I knew Liz and liked her a lot, but the jury was still out on Lori of Self-Defense fame. Linda, Teesa, and Felicia made up the other three-woman room, though Frosty was on her last legs and got thrown out two weeks into second semester for disciplinary problems. She tended to drink too much and was a bit free with sexual favors.

Felicia was in the wrong place. She should have had someone tell her back before R-day, as my brother Paul had told me, "If you want to party and have fun, go to a regular college." Felicia had a very healthy sexual appetite. She would have made a great Oprah show: "What Happens When You Are A Young Woman With Frosted Hair Who Needs It In A College With 4,000 Males (Most of Whom Are Immature)." This isn't to say that other female cadets didn't have sexual tendencies. But as with all things, there are different levels. Some of us, the ones who had nuns and/or heavy duty guilt complexes, were able to follow the rules and keep Miss Libido in check. Others - the ones who didn't have nuns and/or heavy duty guilt complexes- opted not to follow the rules, and took the big risk of getting caught. Even if you weren't caught, your reputation was shot, but you weren't thinking about your reputation. You weren't thinking at all. The male organ or the female heart, hormones and desire, were doing all the thinking. Then there was the last group, a smaller, more rambunctious crew; they'd operated in orbits away from nuns growing up. They walked around the block so they didn't see the convent. They were the ones doing it in the barracks, in broom closets, in empty rooms, and really not making great attempts to hide it.

In the fall, Felicia returned from a trip section very late one Saturday night, reeking of beer, very wasted. The cadets she was with on the trip carried her up the stairs. I wondered how many of them had been under that dress grey. She passed out, doing damage to her eyes; her contacts had stayed in too long. The doctors put big white bandages over both of her eyes so she looked like Mr. Ed, the horse, and Lori, her very sympathetic roommate, the un-Florence Nightingale, was appointed her seeing- eye dog. Big mistake. Felicia was lucky Lori was feeling generous when she took her near those fifth floor steps. As it was, Lori just sent her into walls and furniture. "Hey, she deserves it!" Lori would explain. "The dumb ass didn't take the contacts out because she got drunk!" And who could argue with Lori anyway?! The situation was funnier than it should have been.

Icicles dangled from the windows *inside* our room. I kid you not. Crusts of ice coated the ledge beneath the windows *inside* our room. The heat didn't work. It was like saying the days, calling the minutes, wearing a uniform, the nuisances of West Point that came with the place. We didn't want to make waves about anything; we wanted to fit in, so we drove on, and wore our full sweat suits, parkas and knit caps to bed at night.

If I could market that blind obedience we had, and sell it to parents of teenagers, I'd be a millionaire.

My heart was just not into cheering for basketball. That tomato to the head probably didn't help any. I decided to play company intramurals and I joined Linda, Liz and Teesa on the courts of friendly strife in the volleyball gym. For about two days.

This may not be official, but I can say, with some certainty, that I set an academy record. I don't believe that in the history of the United States Military Academy, there has ever been a cadet who was kicked off intramural volleyball.

Cadet Stranko felt bad. I could tell. He called me over after my second practice. He was the C-I-C for our F-2 team and he'd been in my Beast company as well, so he knew what a sad-sack I was.

He put his clipboard on the bleachers, then turned to face me. He bit his lip and shook his head. "Cadet O'Sullivan, I don't know what to tell you. We need to remove you from the volleyball team."

Whoa. Big kick to the gut! Same spot that was kicked when they told me I was a potential bolo. Building that character.

I walked dejectedly, head hung low—it almost had a permanent spot to hang down to—down the black winding steps in Arvin Gymnasium to the Strength Development room. That's where Cadet Stranko recommended I go: To Strength Development. Strength Development was where the weight lifters and the losers were. The cadets in the weight room were either mammoth, hulk-like with big leather belts around their waist, or they were puny, scrawny and in dire need of remedial training in the fitness arena. I entered that weight lifting room, so embarrassed, so ashamed.

Who would know that getting kicked off that intramural volleyball team would end up being one of the best things that would happen to me while at West Point?

What a difference one upperclassman can make in the life of the plebe whose self-esteem was shot to smithereens. The cadet-in-charge of the Strength Development intramural was good looking, smart, and funny. Cadet Hedge designed a weight training program for me, but left me on my own to work out. On the first day, after I'd completed the circuit training, I asked him if I could go run. He said, "Sure." Like Forrest Gump, I've been running ever since.

I got away; I was alone. It was my escape. The scenery was beautiful. No one bothered me. Soon, I had to run daily. The fact that I was an average runner and was only getting better added fuel to my fire. It's easy to get hooked on something that you like and something you're good at. I was addicted.

Parades were such a bother! We alternated: we did intramurals one day, parades the next. Thanks to rabble-rousing, I hadn't marched in parades during the fall and I hadn't realized what a pain they were. The one good thing was that since we lined up by height, the short people were together and I got to hear Linda's jokes. They were awful. Incredibly, those handsome cadets, marching so magnificently and looking so polished and professional to me when I was a kid, were actually out there telling jokes. I couldn't believe it. We were marching out of the sally-port during my first parade practice with the company, when Cadet Neighbors said to Linda, "West, you got any jokes?"

Linda was prepared. Sort of. In a Linda way. She had a subscription to the Readers' Digest and she really thought those jokes were funny. The upperclassmen were expecting something a bit more racy, but Linda, undaunted, continued to provide her Readers' Digest humor throughout plebe year. Don't you have to just love this kid?

Put a conscientious, over-achieving nerd in an environment like West Point, where performance dictates success, and you can create a seriously obsessive-compulsive psycho. That was me. By Spring break, I was over the edge with both studying and running. You had to do some of both to graduate. I took it to the next level. If there was a world beyond my own little plebe year, I didn't see it. Linda did. She was normal. On Sunday afternoons, when I sat at my desk writing a paper that was due in two weeks, Linda lay on her bed, ignoring her physics problems due the next day, and cutting out china patterns from the NY Times advertisements. On school nights, we'd both sit quietly at our desks, facing the walls, back to back, until I'd hear her flipping through the photos on her desk, getting out gum, groaning about calculus. She'd want to talk. I'd ignore her.

Smell the roses? What roses? Can you say self-centered? I was a woman possessed. I stretched my hamstrings while studying; I shined my shoes while reading the paper. I never read a fun magazine nor watched "Mork and Mindy." My father had always preached "All things in moderation", but I was in my *Don't-Listen-to Anyone-I-Know-Everything* stage of life. Do we ever come out of that stage?

Gail (*left*) and her mother, Plebe-Parent Weekend. April 1978

Spring break gave the girls in F-2 the perfect setting to try to help me be normal. All the upperclassmen left and the plebes had free roam of the campus for the week. We could act like real people. The simple pleasures! We could fall out; we didn't have to walk at attention. We could talk outside, in the hallways, at the tables in the mess hall. We got a taste of the freedoms that would be ours after Recognition during Graduation Week, the last week in May, right around the corner. We liked it.

Back in those days, plebe-parent weekend was held during spring break, so our parents watched us parade, visited us in the barracks, and wore long shimmery dresses and wide lapelled suits for the banquet in the mess hall. My parents and my Aunt Rita and Uncle Gerard drove in; Linda's parents flew from Germany and her grandmother came from Florida. Everywhere you turned on post that weekend, you were smacked head on with pride. Parents' chests were popping and we plebes were feeling pretty good about ourselves for the first time since before R-Day.

Gail (*left*) and Patty Mahoney, Plebe-Parent Weekend. April 1978

Dressed in their finery: (*back row, left to right*) Teesa, Lori, Linda; (*front row, left to right*) Liz and Gail. 1978

I should have been footloose and fancy free, but one awful night put me through the ringer and made me confront reality quick. It was the first time that I was faced with an honor code dilemma. Tell the truth and get my roommates in trouble? Or lie. I had no time to remember the lectures from Beast. I had no time to think about the repercussions.

Liz had become friends with a firstie in our company. She worked with him on the 100th Night Show, a performance put on by the first class one hundred nights before their graduation. Cadet Flowers was going to Florida on Spring break, and had asked Liz to do him a favor when he was away. He asked her to take care of his bird.

Cadet regulations allowed us to have one picture on our desk, one poster on the back of the door and one stereo per room (after Christmas, for plebes). Those regulations didn't mention any pets. Granted F-2 was known as "The Zoo", a nickname it had earned in the '60s and had maintained with pride. Captain DiBella had been charged with the dubious task of eradicating the nickname, but this proved to be impossible. Besides confirming the company's reputation for having a good time, the nickname aroused pride and cohesiveness, but it did not allow its cadet members to house animals.

The bird was not Airborne. So, it wasn't as much of a pet as a mercy mission. Flowers had found the tiny injured thing near the barracks and was nursing it back to health in a box in his miscellaneous drawer, under his wardrobe, the same place I kept my oat bran. Tuesday night, Liz and Lori left the room to go feed the bird. Whenever we left our rooms, we had to mark our cards. In those days, hanging on the wall just inside every cadet room was a plastic card, marked with our name and a dismal new cadet picture. Our photos were taken when we exited the pool in the summer and so, our pictures reflected drowned, scared, bald rats. If you were in your room, the card had to be on the space marked "Unmarked." If you were not in your room, but in an authorized place like the latrine or... the latrine (plebes weren't allowed many other places), the card had to be marked "Authorized Absence." If you marked your card "Authorized Absence" and then went to a place you knew you were not supposed to be, you were lying. You just committed an honor violation. Good bye, West Point. Hello, Boston College. So, if you were going somewhere you weren't supposed to be, but didn't want to commit an honor violation, you left your card "Unmarked." This meant you committed a regulations violation (you weren't in your room when your card was "unmarked"), but you had not committed an honor violation because you didn't lie about where you were. It wasn't as complicated as it sounds. Liz and Lori were not authorized to be in the upperclassman's room feeding the bird so they didn't mark their cards when they left that Tuesday night.

They were only gone a few minutes. I was reading quietly at my desk. "Knock, Knock." This is not good, I think. There are no upperclassmen around. Must be the Tac making some sort of unannounced check.

"Come in, Sir."

This is really not good. It was not the Tac. It was the OC. The officer-in-charge, an officer whose job was to make sure cadet life was being lived by the rules and regulations, which, at this time, on the fifth floor of Central Barracks, was not the case.

The OC looked at the card on the wall and looked at me.

"How are you tonight, O'Sullivan?"

"Fine, Sir."

"Where are your roommates, O'Sullivan?"

"Ummmmmmmmmmm. Sir, may I make a statement?"

"Yes, I asked you a question. Where are your roommates?"

This was not heading in a good direction. Rat or lie, neither very good options. So I scrambled for more time.

"Sir, they are down the hall."

"Doing what, O'Sullivan?"

"Sir, they are down the hall..." The time for the truth had arrived. It was inevitable. I couldn't delay any longer. I paused. In the softest, lowest voice I could find, "They are feeding the bird."

"What?"

"Sir, they are...feeding the bird..."

"O'Sullivan, what did you say?"

And resignedly, "Sir, they are.. feeding the bird."

The OC required some further explanation. Liz and Lori didn't get in trouble. Cadet Flowers did. Keeping an animal in the zoo was against all regulations, but asking a plebe to knowingly violate a regulation was a more serious offense. The bird was booted, but the F-2 Zoo stayed alive.

> **"The reward of a thing well done is to have done it."**
>
> —Ralph Waldo Emerson

It finally came, that light at the end of that very long tunnel. The Class of 1978 would graduate and be commissioned second lieutenants in the Army. I actually didn't care very much about that. What I cared about was Recognition.

Recognition. We had lived for this day since R-Day, almost eleven months earlier, when we'd been stripped of our identity and every day since, been considered a non-person by the three upperclasses. Now, after the Graduation parade, we would be recognized as people again. The upperclass would shake our hands and acknowledge us as fellow upperclassmen. We had endured our plebe year.

Before it happened, the upperclass felt a moral obligation to bring their harassment to a higher level one last time. Minute callers took the first wave of the attack. Plebe uniforms took a hit. The upperclassmen tarnished our belt buckles, smudged our shoes, knocked our hats askew. Incredibly, there were even those particularly abusive upperclassmen who removed the breastplate from the uniform of the minute caller to wham it with his rifle butt. These were the men who, as youths, were pimply faced and outcast, who mutilated Barbie dolls and colored their severed limbs with ketchup, who lived to torture live frogs. The admissions process is comprehensive, but didn't ask these questions.

Formation out in the area was a farce as the hazing continued in the faces of plebes who long ago had lost that vulnerability. For some plebes, this harassment led to anger as they realized that in minutes, they would be able to engage quasi-legally in some form of fisticuffs. The cadet I later married told an upperclassman, "As soon as I'm Recognized, I'm going to kick your ass!" But for most of us, this harassment, no matter how severe, could not touch us. We were about to be Recognized. We were about to be officially done with the longest year of our lives.

To the first classmen, the Graduation parade was a final tribute to four years of dedication, the end of a cadet career, and the beginning of a career of service to our nation. They had, four years earlier, marched towards the corps in their Acceptance Day parade. Now, in the Graduation parade, they separated themselves and marched away from the corps. It may have been full of significance to the firsties, but to the plebes, the Graduation parade was but a necessary prelude to Recognition. As the companies left the apron and marched back through the sally ports after the parade, all hell broke loose. The echoes in the sally ports were deafening.

They told us to line up, all the plebes, shoulder to shoulder. They told us to take off our tall "tar-bucket" parade hats and stand at ease. Then they marched through, all the upperclassmen, by class, one by one. They shook our hands; they called us by our first name; they told us their first name. Cadet Kelly, our first company commander, led the ranks through and as he shook my hand and said, "Congratulations, Gail," I was overwhelmed. I refused to get emotional. The relief, the feeling of accomplishment, knowing that I did what no one thought I could do, put me on the verge of tears. Short-lived enthusiasm as soon, down the line, walked Cadet Disher. Hard to even look him in the face, never mind get excited about shaking his greasy hand. But then, Cadet Damsel. Such a nice guy. My eyes watered as he offered his congratulations with such sincerity. Cadet Hedge, my strength development mentor, who had helped me salvage some of my physical fitness self-esteem. Cadet Garcia, who majored in English and took special pride in my academic achievements. Cadet Meyer, who had walked the Fish Eaters to Wednesday night mass during the summer, and who, in F-2, had always smiled, always been concerned. We were similar, with brown hair and eyes and our slight builds. He stood in front of me with his trademark wide grin; he opened his arms wide and embraced me with a big bear hug. "My little sister! You remind me so much of my little sister!" That was it. Put me over the edge. My eyes watered to the brim.

I was recognized. I finished plebe year. Maybe Sister Agnesca was right after all. Maybe I could do this.

eight

Camp Buckner

(Best Summer of My Life?)

"You can never go home again."

—Thomas Wolfe

Did Wolfe go away to college? A military school, recognized by only a few from a different generation who spent most of their days at Henry's Pub, and not understood by a single one of his high school pals?

I loved going home, but something was different. I figured it was me.

They gave us two weeks of leave between graduation and Camp Buckner, our next scheduled fun activity, and Cape Cod was calling. When I was in high school, my parents splurged and spent the big bucks on a mobile home (we couldn't call it a trailer in front of my mother), in a buggy, pine-blanketed park on a pond full of tadpoles and ice water, in Mashpee. This was the summer my friends drank their way through Happy Hours on the Cape. When I was squaring corners and saying the Days, they'd left Brigham's Specials for Margueritas. The drinking age in the late '70s was eighteen, so they were legal and fun.

It could be said that I was *not* fun. I went with them to one Happy Hour at a club in Yarmouth, and felt like a nun in full habit at a Led Zeppelin concert, so out of place it hurt. Plus, they hung out with my old boyfriend's crowd. Talk about awkward. I didn't drink, didn't have anything in common with my old friends, didn't have a boyfriend, and didn't look good. These facts severely limited my summer options. I slept, read trashy magazines, focused on my tan, and slept some more.

When I reported in late June to Second Company, King of the Hill, I didn't buy the local propaganda that advertised Buckner to be "the best summer of my life." They'd said the same thing about Lake Frederick. Sleeping on the ground, Infantry tactics through the woods all day, and thinking that a porta-potty was a special treat was just not me. Camp Buckner promised more of the same, lots more. Seven weeks more. I preferred hotels.

Second Company was one of eight companies, Quonset huts like on "Gomer Pyle," scattered around Lake Popolopen, eight miles down the road from West Point. Back then, all the women were housed in one barracks. You could come in the door at one end of the hut, walk through the female bay of bunk beds, girls sitting on their footlockers writing letters home, reading magazines, past the female latrine, lavender lotions, fruity shampoos, then out past the other female bay. The male barracks was built the same way. You'd pass the male bay, guys napping on their bunks with one hand stuck down their waistband, a string of drool down their chins, past the male latrine, heavy urine odors, then past the other male bay. The excitement of the summer was the streakers who ran through the female barracks at night wearing only goose bumps, combat boots, and gas masks.

Camp Buckner was designed to teach us about the real Army and since I knew more about nuclear physics than I did about the Army, I decided it would be good to pay attention. One of the girls in my squad was like me, poor thing. We'd been rabble-rousers together. Becky was a nice girl, too sweet to be at West Point. The other girl, Karen, was wiry and hard, had been to college for a few years, and was more competitive than Becky and me put together and then some. The guys, except for the required screwball, were fun and easygoing. Timmy was a cute blond from Revere, back home, so, in accordance with the pattern I had established early on, I developed a crush on him. I didn't expect much though. Camouflage paint smeared all over my face did nothing for me.

I got along with everyone. If I had to write a list of names of people I really didn't like, it would honestly be blank. I even liked Karen. She wasn't someone I'd want to have with me if I needed a hug, but she'd be awesome to be stranded with on a deserted island. I'm sure she'd keep me alive. If I had to write a list of names of people I sort of didn't like it would only have one person on it. My Buckner platoon leader. He was a guy in the Class of '80 and very good looking. He knew it. Humility is a trait I have always greatly respected and this guy reeked of arrogance and self-confidence. I just kept to myself, talked to him as infrequently as possible, ignored him and didn't think anything of it.

Then he counseled me. He had to counsel everyone in the platoon. It was his job. I sat with him outside the barracks and he cracked some dumb joke and I thought to myself I can't believe this guy gets to write a counseling statement on me. I didn't laugh at his joke.

I listened to him tell me my good points. They always do that first, almost like serving the dessert before the burned meatloaf which I have tried on my family and found that no one eats the burned meatloaf either way, before the cake or after, so why bother with the good points first. He paused and looked, for the first time in the three weeks I'd known him, uncomfortable.

"OK," he said. He was suddenly serious, almost looking wounded. "I can tell you don't like me."

My eyes shot wide.

He continued. "Listen, that's OK. You don't have to like everyone. And I don't know much about leadership, but I do know this. If you have a boss you don't like, and I've been your boss out here, you have to learn to fake it better."

If I'd had any guts at all (no roller coasters), I would have responded with "Then stop acting so damn arrogant", but, of course, I was stunned. I sat on the steps, looking down at my sneakers. I shook my head slightly, as if to nod—what, agreement?—then, mumbled a hushed "OK." He wished me good luck in yearling year and pulled himself up to leave me feeling rotten. I still didn't like him, but I felt terrible that he knew I didn't like him. The only solace was in the fact that he lived over in third regiment. I figured I'd never see him again.

The training was unlike anything your average college sophomore experiences. We blew up bridges. This was cool, though I didn't get the thrill out of it that the guys seemed to get. Males are just genetically designed to want to blow things up and make farting noises with their underarms. Firing big guns was also cool. Soldiers from the 82nd Airborne division were assigned to West Point for the summer to conduct our training and most had never worked with women soldiers before so I was selected, as the scrawny one, to fire the light anti-tank weapon, a tube-like thing that sat on your shoulders, and made a very, very, very loud noise. They gave me ear plugs and I put them in, but Miss Nosey Britches was afraid she'd miss something. When you're already one step behind everyone else, you need to be able to hear so that you can catch up. I wore the ear plugs, but loosely. It turned out to be a bad decision, one that caused worry my firstie year, one that I live with daily, still.

The highlight of our Buckner summer was the Ft. Knox trip. Located in Kentucky, one of the forty eight states I'd never been in, Ft. Knox was the home of Armor and we were going to learn all about tanks, just in case I hadn't read the book I got for Christmas the year before, which I hadn't. I was more excited about the fact that I'd fly on an airplane for the very first time. Even if it was a monstrous, green military plane whose belly we crawled into via a big garage door at the butt, to sit crunched together on some sort of netting, wearing ear plugs, no sodas, no peanuts, it was still a very big deal to me. And driving the tank was like being in a real-live amusement park, until I hit a wall of rocks, broke a track, had to be towed, and then endured the female driver cracks for a week.

Until Recondo training, Buckner wasn't all that bad. Recondo: three night-less days, hour after hour of infantry tactics, leading patrols, getting ambushed, no showers, no hot food, no toilets, no sleep. Before we got to that fun, though, we faced the infamous Recondo Run, two miles of rocky trails that were so steep, you literally had to crawl, in full gear, combat boots, steel pot, rucksack, carrying your M-16. It was the hardest thing I did at West Point, including Indoor Obstacle Courses, electrical engineering term-end exams and dating a cadet. It was total misery.

We started with a partner though we didn't have to finish with him. They tried that the year before. They'd forced bonding in the Class of '80 and re-quired the teams to finish together which led to women being yanked by their teeth or hair or whatever their tired, frustrated partner, could find to yank, so they nixed the "Finish Together" rule for our class. Bill was a good friend in my squad; over six feet tall, a football player from Tennessee, and we both figured I'd have no problem. The morning PT runs at Buckner were hard and hilly, but I'd done OK and even gained a reputation of sorts as a runner, which was ironic, considering my background as a cheerleader who'd been kicked off intramural volleyball.

To say I overestimated my abilities would be a gross understatement.

We stood at the start together and Bill looked down at me with his brown eyes, assuring me without a word. The cadet who was timing us said "GO" and we ran. Or, Bill ran. I ran about three steps, then my legs, so over-whelmed with the weight of the gear, down-shifted into a shuffle. Bill slowed to wait for me. Less than fifty yards from the start, a huge tree lay across our path and as I followed Bill, who had so gracefully hopped over it, my total and complete lack of coordination did me in. I misjudged the height of the fallen tree and my foot didn't clear it. I flew into it, then over it, and landed hard, face first, with a heavy thud. The rim of my helmet hit the trail first, but the rest of me followed and the backpack crushed me into the dirt, onto my M-16 which hurt. A lot. Bill helped me up. I tried to catch my breath and we began to run again, but that nose-dive and the weight of that gear on my pathetic frame were too much for me. Near the mid-way point, Bill begrudgingly left me so that he could pass, as it was clear that I was dying alive, and I chugged along, alone, dry heaving and sucking wind. I failed the run.

All the girls, except Karen, no shocker there, and a few of the guys as well, failed the first run and woke up before everyone else the next morning, crawled out of our shelter-halves in the cold dark woods, and loaded the Loser truck. *Should I just reserve a seat on these trucks?* They dropped us off near the start. We trudged along the dirt road looking down, watching our step, anxious to just be done with this miserable course. This was our last chance to pass. I was ready mentally for the weight of the equipment and I passed and salvaged a bit of self-esteem. Becky didn't pass. Those of us who passed didn't know what to say, so no one said a word. They trucked us back, our sweat starting to make us shiver, to our bivouac site. No one was there. The rest of the company, the ones who passed the run the first time, the squared away, competent ones, left the losers behind. They'd packed up and marched to the next training site. Only one shelter half stood on the site. Becky, Karen and I had shared a tent and Karen hadn't taken the tent down. My eyes watered. That lone tent stood shouting to Becky and me that we didn't belong, that we couldn't hang with the others. We tore it down and packed it up and caught up with our company. I seemed to spend most of my time at West Point trying to catch up.

I had to prove that I belonged. I had to earn the Recondo patch. I wanted it more than anything. In my mind, if I got that patch, it would prove that I deserved to be there, that I belonged. To get the patch, you had to pass the run and pass the patrols, and before we even started the patrols, I was not feeling very Hooah. (Hooah was a term used for hard charging, gung-ho military). The night before the patrols started, all the yearlings in First and Second Company, about two hundred of us, sat on faded, peeling bleachers and listened to a grizzly, mafia-looking, non-commissioned officer (NCO) shout at us ways to survive in the wilderness. As I squashed mosquitoes and swung at gnats, I started to wonder about this whole thing. After three more years at this place, I'd be eating bugs to survive? Is this my future?

It got worse. They gave each squad—there were about ten of us in a squad- a live chicken and a bag of vegetables. This was dinner. The chicken was intended to meet his maker soon. The idea was that we'd have chicken stew (and not from a can) for dinner. The macho thing was to bite the head off the live chicken. That killed the chicken, and I'm assuming it also left a disgusting taste and a feather or two in your mouth. The NCO demonstrated. I almost threw up. He asked for volunteers and Jen, a no-nonsense blue-eyed blond basketball player, succumbing to peer pressure and that insatiable desire to earn the respect of our male peers, climbed down from the bleachers and bit the head off. Danny, one of the guys in my squad, teased me to do it. "Yeah, right," I responded. "Give me the vegetables. I'll chop."

It was pitch black when we left that training site and walked back to our bivouac area. I walked along the trail with Becky, following the cat eyes, small patches that lit up in the dark on the helmets in front of us.

"I don't know about all this," I told her. "If this is the Army, I may be at the wrong place."

She agreed. We were too tired to talk about it. We just kept walking.

When we arrived back to the bivouac site, I scuffed over to the water buffalo in the dark to brush my teeth and I felt a figure standing beside me. The water from the spigot was cupped in my hand and I was about to gulp and spit when I realized the dark figure was our company tactical officer. I'd never talked to him before.

"Cadet O'Sullivan, come over here for a minute, please."

Oh, oh, now what. Have they identified me as a potential bolo?

"I was behind you walking back here. I heard you talking to your roommate."

Shoot. I know I was whining….

"I want to tell you that you will not be doing this stuff in the Army. This is Infantry tactics. Women are not allowed to branch Infantry. You're doing a great job and I don't want you to get discouraged from all this. Just continue to do what you're doing."

I think, *Wow, nice guy.* (I like anyone who compliments me!) *But that's good news about not doing this in the Army. Sure, I'll drive on.*

I say, "Yes, Sir."

(Years later, marching through the woods in Germany protecting the Fulda Gap from hordes of communists, shivering, exhausted, dirty, and hungry, I thought about how that nice tactical officer was full of bologna.)

He told me, "Good luck on the patrols tonight. Go get some rest."

I slept for a few hours before the first patrol began. They merged together in one never-ending, sleepless, cold, hot, wretched stretch of time. The nights were freezing; the days were stifling hot. An NCO, with squinty eyes, tattooed forearms, and a crew cut so short he looked bald, and a cadet, a big, round-faced, quiet first classman who was assigned to the Recondo committee, marched quietly through the woods with our squad. The NCO picked one of us to be the patrol leader and one of us to be the assistant patrol leader and they led us off into the woods, toward the objective, in bounding over-watch, to wait to be ambushed by the opposing forces. There was no rest, no sleep. After one ambush, we gathered, the NCO told the patrol leader what he'd done wrong, then he chose another patrol leader, who took out his compass and pointed us in a new direction and we began to walk again. After twenty four hours, we walked into trees. We ate dry cocoa powder from our C-rations to stay awake.

There was one M-60 machine gun per squad. Our individual weapon, the M-16, seven and a half pounds unloaded, was a drop in the bucket compared to the M-60, twenty-three pounds unloaded. With the rucksack and the steel pot, the equipment was more than a third of my weight though I wasn't doing math in my head as much as regretting the incredibly puniness of my upper body. The guys rotated the M-60 between them, taking turns carrying it across their front, with their M-16 strapped down their back, next to their rucksack. After the second day, all the guys had carried the M-60. More than anything else, I hated to volunteer, but what choice did I have. They all said no, it was ok, they could carry it again; I didn't have to do it. They were such good guys. Their cheeks were greased with camouflaged sweat and their eyes were barely open. It was only fair. It was pitch dark, 2:00 a.m., and Mark disengaged himself from the weapon and gave it to me and it weighed about fifteen tons heavier than I thought it would and I tried to lift up my feet, to not make noises in the leaves as I followed the cat eyes on Danny's steel pot, ten meters ahead of me. The next closest guy was ten meters behind me (so we all didn't get wasted by one hand grenade). My hair felt like gasoline, smeared into my scalp, my bones were hollow, drained, aching more with every step. I'd never been more miserable in my life. I thought: No one will see me. I thought: It's coming anyway. I can't stop it. And I cried silently, trudging along, one foot in front of the other.

I carried that M-60 because it wasn't fair not to. I figured it was my duty as a member of that squad. I *barely* carried it. The guys in my squad felt so bad for me; they took it back the second that patrol was over while we were being out-briefed by SFC Rock. I didn't argue.

Twenty-two years after my Camp Buckner experience, John, a classmate, introduced me to his wife outside the school playground where our kids were playing. "Joan," he said, "This is Gail. She was in my Buckner squad and she carried the M-60." Twenty-three years later, my husband played in an alumni-rugby game and I stood on the sidelines to watch the game, the good wife of a man who refuses to admit he's aging. He jogged over to me pointing behind him to the old players on the field, "Hey, Dave is here. He's your classmate. Said he was in your Buckner squad and you carried the M-60."

Three things cross my mind: First, I'm sure glad they didn't see me crying. That would have ruined my rep. And second, if I'd known it was such a big deal to them, I would have tried to carry it longer. Or maybe argued a little when they took it away from me. Or at least not jumped for joy when it left my arms. And third, I wondered if this happens to all female cadets. I wonder if the actions or inactions of today's cadets will stay with their classmates for years. I have a feeling that it will.

Recondo ended with the Slide for Life, a rope device hung high over Lake Popolopen that you slid down, hanging on for dear life, then released one hand to salute which meant hanging on with one hand, which meant falling into the water fifteen feet below, and then, it was over; we were done. We trudged back up the hill, weighed down by the lake water, bone-tired from the past week, and then cadets started saying that the Recondo Patch ceremony was in an hour, but if you didn't get the patch, you stayed in the barracks and cleaned them. This place really made the losers feel good. No patch, pick up the Ajax and scrub the showers.

There were only four girls in our bay of twenty who passed the run. I showered, feeling bad about the girls who had to stay and clean, put my uniform on and walked outside with Karen to find out where the ceremony was. Our cadet company commander, a burly football player in the Class of 1979 who cared and was kind, called me over. He didn't look good.

"Gail," he started. I knew something was up. His cheeks were pinched in, like he didn't want to tell me something. Did my parents die?

"You don't have to go to the ceremony."

I looked up at him, confused.

He paused. Finally, he said, "You didn't get your patch."

I cried in front of people twice when I was at West Point. This was one of them.

I didn't get it. I managed to ask him why. He looked like he wished he could crawl into a hole; I'm sure I was his first sobbing female leadership opportunity. I wasn't convulsing, but those tears overflowed in a constant, steady stream down my red, sunken-in cheeks.

"I don't know. Your name just isn't on the list. You must have failed your patrol. Did they tell you that you failed?"

"No," I replied. I rubbed my eyes to stop the crying. I told him OK. Thanks for telling me. I wiped the tears, turned around, and walked back to the barracks. I scrubbed the showers.

My parents had driven from Boston to take Linda and me home for the weekend. Our first and only pass for the summer would be spent sleeping. My mother hugged me, her face full of concern and worry. I'd lost weight and looked like an emaciated Bambi who just found out her mother was shot, wide-eyed and so sad. Linda and I tumbled wearily into the back seat and my mother asked innocently, "Honey, what's this about a Recondo patch?"

I lost it and this time it was those convulsive, full body sobs you see in the movies. Poor Mom felt bad for asking, felt bad for me being at this place and looking so awful, and didn't feel any better about it—for years. Linda and I both fell asleep before the car was out of the parking lot. We woke up screaming as my dad was pulling up to my house, four hours later. There were tall bushes, lining both sides of the driveway, and we'd had the same nightmare. We were being ambushed. When Linda and I finally got up around noon for breakfast the next morning, catalogs from Holy Cross were sitting on the kitchen table. This was the first time my parents were visibly shaken. I looked bad, my self-esteem was at an all-time low, and they just weren't sure I was doing the right thing. What they didn't understand is that when you're nineteen years old, if your parents think you may not be doing the right thing; for some reason, that pushes you harder into doing it. This phenomenon happens to all nineteen year olds. I wasn't even close to being a rebel. I was just stubborn and pig headed.

"Stop," I said to them. "It's fine. I'll gain the weight back. I'll get over the stupid patch."

I did neither, but my parents did stop bugging me. I'm sure they never stopped worrying though.

I was a fairly considerate, mature high school student who sent cards to grandmothers on their birthdays, but I never thought about what my parents went through from R-Day on. Now, as a mother, I cannot imagine sending a squared away child, never mind a ninety-five pound, clueless daughter into the second class of women at a military academy. No wonder my mother tried to convince herself on R-day that I was tough as nails. She was scared to death! And I was so into my own adventure, so independent and close-hold with my emotions, I didn't make it any easier on her.

Years later, when I was a lieutenant in the Army, I learned why I didn't get that Recondo patch. Linda got married at Ft. Leavenworth, Kansas and I flew to the wedding to be a bridesmaid. The best man, a 1979 graduate, looked familiar and we started the "what company were you in" conversation, but he knew instantly where he remembered me from. He'd been that firstie assigned to our Buckner squad and he recounted the whole story over roast beef at the rehearsal dinner at the Fort Leavenworth Officers' Club. He told me that SFC Rock just said no, I was too small; I didn't look like I should be wearing a Recondo patch. This reeked of sexual discrimination, but even worse, I realized this was my fault. Why didn't I ever ask the question why? Why hadn't I asked my tactical officer to find out why I didn't get that patch? Waves! I was so afraid of making waves, I got crushed by them.

I had always thought that not getting that Recondo patch was the only outward demonstration of sexual discrimination I experienced at West Point. More than twenty years after graduation, a huge hole was shot in that theory. Will, a classmate, a varsity athlete while at West Point, aviation brigade commander during Iraqi Freedom, is an old friend of my husband's from flight school days. We were eating chips and salsa and telling old stories while our kids played in the pool, and my husband said to him, "Hey, you didn't get your Recondo patch, did you?"

His face fell. I know that fall!

"What happened?" I asked.

"I really don't know," he replied. "I never found out why. Failed my patrol, I guess, but no one told me why. I was devastated." He paused. "You know, I know it wasn't a big deal, but it's why I didn't go Infantry or to Ranger school."

I shared his pain. We'd both been ripped off. And I realized something. The reason why I didn't get the patch was not necessarily because I was a scrawny female. The reason why I didn't get that patch is because life's not fair. Sometimes we can blame life's inequities on sex, race, or religion. But sometimes, life is just plain old not fair.

nine

Yearling Year

*"I have never let my schooling
interfere with my education."*

—Mark Twain

Sophomores at West Point are called "yearlings." The name fits. A yearling, a one-year-old animal, is not a baby anymore, but not ready to go solo yet either. A yearling is a work still in progress. I use this analogy. Lock someone up for about a year. Don't let him out. Then, eleven months later, yank him out of the playpen, call him by his first name, let him walk with his hands uncupped, and throw him in the woods for two months with a thousand other kids who were also just yanked out of their playpens. Call him a yearling. Then, put him in charge of a new baby, too. You *do* want the kid to be a leader someday.

Yearlings often don't handle their new freedom well. They have trouble focusing. They have a lot of fun. They do dumb things. They act on any dare thrown their way by any numbskull. They throw live animals out of barracks windows with home-made parachutes; they fill old iced tea bottles with wine and guzzle them; they light floors on fire with charcoal lighter. Yearlings have to re-learn those "people skills" their mothers made sure they left home with, all over again, so that by their cow summer, one full year after Camp Buckner, they are *almost* real people again.

✦ ✦ ✦ ✦

I was a work in progress all yearling year. Mentors, parents, people who cared about me, drowned me in advice. But I already knew everything! I knew who I wanted to be and what kind of person I would not be; so, their advice went *Whoosh* by my ears (though I did nod and smile politely). Sometimes when you think you know something, you really don't know anything at all.

✦ ✦ ✦ ✦

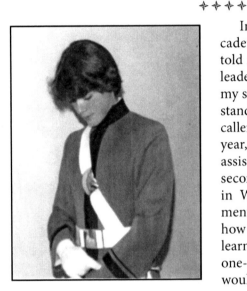

Gail preparing for guard detail

In September, I was given my first cadet leadership opportunity. They told me I would be an assistant squad leader. Although I would like to think my selection was based upon my outstanding performance as head minute caller during re-orgy week of my plebe year, the fact is all yearlings serve as assistant squad leaders, either first or second semester. This is the first step in West Point's leadership development system. Plebe year, cadets learn how to follow. Yearling year, cadets learn leadership with a one-on-one or one-on-two leadership opportunity. I would be personally responsible for two whole plebes, night and day. One was a gangly, goofy kid; the other was a hunk of a varsity football player.

This is how I prepared for my leadership challenge. I went to CVS and bought posters and magic markers. Over Labor Day weekend, home in Braintree, I spent Saturday afternoon creating two posters. On glow in the dark orange poster board, I drew a pie, divided into pieces that represented, in cheerful neon colors, the knowledge that my charges were required to pass off. On the other yellow poster (bright! *Let's be happy*, I seemed to be shouting!) was a matrix with physical fitness requirements that they had to master. The posters were hung up in the hallway outside my room and I was rather proud of them. They took a lot of work!

A new tactical officer had been assigned to Company F-2 over the summer. Army personnel usually rotate every two to three years and so Captain DiBella had moved on to another assignment and his replacement was Major Jackson Henry Lowe, a 1965 West Point grad, hard-charger, straight-ar-row. Tall and rugged-looking, with a blond crew cut, black-rimmed military glasses, and a concerned forehead, Major Lowe roamed the hallways of the barracks morning, noon and night, either trying to get to know us, or trying to show us who was in charge, probably both. I was outside my room in the hall-way, coloring in "The Corps" which Gillis had just passed off, when Major Lowe walked up to my poster. He just stared. I stopped coloring. Finally, he asked, "Cadet O'Sullivan?" Like Cadet O'Dowd, he managed to say things without say-ing them, and I knew he was saying, *Please explain what this rainbow pie is?*

I explained the purpose of both charts proudly, like a new mother ex-plaining how she'd keep track of how much formula her baby had and what size bowel movements followed, and he just shook his head like Cadet O'Dowd used to do.

As an assistant squad leader, I tried to be stern and professional, but it was hard. Gillis, the football player, was adorable. He smiled too much. At me. Initially, I wasn't sure what to do. He was just being a goof ball and I'm sure that he had no romantic inclinations toward his skinny little Northern assistant squad leader; he was a Texan and his one authorized knick-knack was a picture of his big-haired blonde from back home. I put on my best nun attitude, cold and distant, and it worked; he cut the smiling. I didn't want to be so aloof; I liked the fact that he was in such a good mood. But I worried about perceptions. What would someone say if they saw him smil-ing at me? I'd become my mother, afraid of what the neighbors would say.

I never thought about liking Gillis. It was against the rules, for one thing, but the other reason was upbringing. We had certain unwritten rules growing up:

Women dusted; men pushed lawn mowers.

Women didn't call men on the phone; men called women.

Women could go out with older men. This was not only allowed, but was very acceptable.

But women could not go out with younger men. I'm not sure why. My mother was always embarrassed about being six months older than my fa-ther, so I can only assume that this unwritten rule came off the boat from Ireland with the potato farmers.

My other plebe, Fuller, was a tie-up who looked sad doing about every-thing he tried to do and tried not to do. He probably looked sad sleeping. I felt sorry for him really. Even when he called minutes flawlessly in his deliv-ery, his appearance begged for hazing. The upperclassmen had determined they wanted to run him out. This was never said in words; it was said in their attitude, their attention, their overall jerkiness towards him. My gut said *who am I to say this kid doesn't belong here?* Probably because I was such an unlikely cadet myself, I had some empathy for those who unintentionally asked for trouble, like Fuller.

Females were a whole different issue. I'd cut Fuller some slack because West Point was supposed to be a developmental place and maybe with time, he'd figure it out. But the slack rule didn't apply to females. I expected them to carry their own load and more, from R-Day on. My double standard was easy to explain: females had the potential to ruin *my* reputation. I'm here busting *my* butt to try to earn respect and if you can't hang, you'll make us all look bad. This attitude, shared by most females, led to heavy competition among the females, within classes and within the corps, and helps explain some of the hostility I sensed from the Class of '80 women. *I want to look better than you*, we all said to each other. It's too bad someone didn't stop us and say *why don't you all try to look good together?*

We probably wouldn't have listened anyway.

> "There is a single-most common thing shared by most graduates: We learned about, knew and established strong relations with people in groups that changed our lives."
>
> —Classmate, 1981

Spring break, yearling year: A recipe for disaster. The five girls in F-2—Linda, Lori, Liz, Teesa, and me—flew to Florida together. It was a sitcom waiting to be written. The only thing that the five of us had in common was sharing plebe and yearling year in the Zoo, a bond with the strength of steel girders. But personality-wise, take a look at what sat on that plane together: Wild Teesa, the fun-loving blond, who could have a good time in solitary confinement; Normal Liz, the city girl, who tried to add balance to the rest of us; Lori, the stud, whose toughness matched only her wit; Red-headed Linda, the naïve little sister to everyone in F-2, and Sister Gail, the rule-follower, obsessed with running and not eating much.

Some plans always look better a month out.

Together, we spent two days at Linda's grandmother's house in Fort Lauderdale, then the four of us left Linda behind so she could spend more time with Gram, and we drove to Orlando for our big Disney adventure. Liz's boyfriend showed up and surprised her. (Later, she realized that he must have had a girlfriend back home who wasn't around and so he flew to Florida and found Liz.) Teesa had arranged for her boyfriend to meet us and we all went to a nightclub in Orlando, all spiffed up, our first night in town. What was I thinking? Teesa and Liz and their boyfriends began to disco the night away.

The girls in Orlando: (*left to right*) Lori, Liz, a friend, Teesa, Gail

That left Lori and me. Instead of looking at me in my sky-blue gauchos and sky-blue-and-white checkered blazer and ballooning white tie-blouse (it was the '70s and I looked really hot), Lori opted to drink a lot (I look at pictures of that outfit and can't say I blame her). She left the club and went out to sleep in the car. I didn't know a soul, didn't drink, didn't dance much or well. Plus, I looked like a pastel Easter bunny. Planted like the lone cypress against a back wall, thinking about the cost of a two-hour taxi cab (back to the safety of Linda's grandmother's house where socializing skills were not required), I saw a familiar face walking towards my wall. I couldn't believe it. He was smiling and he looked really good. I stood dumbfounded that he was there. It was my Buckner platoon leader.

He wore jeans and a tight off-white shirt and was bronzed from the sun. He did have a killer smile. OK, I thought, I know I don't like this guy, but how soon we forget. We danced, talked, danced and went to Disney the next day.

Back at school after Spring break, I studied and ran, and every once in a while, dated the platoon leader who had told me to not make it so obvious that I hated his guts. Linda didn't like him. She thought he was a womanizer. *Whoosh,* her advice went whizzing past my ears because I knew better; I was changing him into a one-woman man! My parents didn't like him either—*Whoosh,* by the other ear! I felt responsible to continue my good influence on him. We left for our summer training, promising to write to each other. I ended my yearling year, still convinced I could be nice and not aggressive, and certain that I was molding a twenty-year-old man into who *I* wanted him to be.

I left West Point after my yearling year, definitely still a work in progress.

Yearling year, 1978: (*left to right*) Linda, Sharon, Kim, Gail

ten

Duty, Honor, Country and Love

*"The only real training for
leadership is leadership."*

—A. Jay

W est Point is a year-round experience. Long gone are those endless, summer days at the beach, days that rolled over on top of each other and finally, abruptly, crashed into Labor Day and back to school again. At West Point, you do Beast your first summer; you do Buckner your second summer. The first time you have any choice in your summer training is after yearling year. And the amount of choice you have is like when my kids ask me if they can have cocoa puffs for dinner. Catch me in a good mood, with no food in the house, it may happen. But don't count on it.

They've been with us our whole life. In grammar school, they were the kids with the long row of yellow stars next to their name on the chart taped on the wall near the coat rack for all the parents, pointing their long fingers and beaming their proud smiles, to see at the Open House. In high school, they were the kids who gave up their study periods to help the vice-principal patrol the halls, hunting down students wandering without a hall pass. At West Point, they were the cadets who studied and shined their shoes, replaced their heels when they wore out, shaved their heads and had no sideburns, looked like they stepped out of a muscle magazine, always got along with their superiors, sometimes got along with their peers and hardly ever got along with their subordinates. They always followed the rules. They made up more rules! They played the West Point game. We called them "High Rollers." In today's lingo, West Point calls them, more appropriately, "emerging leaders."

Tacs nominated the "High Rollers" so if the Tac didn't get out of his office much, didn't know the personalities; he could select a Dud—an overachiever who wasn't listening to that "Cooperate and Graduate" lecture in Beast. West Point was big on collaboration and teamwork. They force it on you, by default often, during plebe year. Example: Saturday night dinner was optional, which meant that plebes, although required to sit at attention, not talk and eat in little bites, could choose their own seats in the mess hall and not have to endure the constant corrections that came with every other meal. One Saturday night, a group of F-2 plebes sat together and Rick passed the tray of Swiss steak with brown gravy to Nick, who was sitting next to him. Rick suffered a short lapse of coordination and loaded his dress grey jacket with two pieces of Swiss steak and two gallons of brown gravy. The Swiss steak could be put back on the plate, but the brown gravy wasn't going anywhere. His F-2 classmates, forced to hold in their laughter as they sat at attention, realized that Rick would be a sitting duck, a pinging duck, really, walking back through the area wearing this gross uniform violation, dress grey with gravy. Upperclassmen would be all over him like a wet blanket. The plebes couldn't talk until they were back in their rooms. Wordlessly, they formed a tight formation, with Rick as the epicenter, then pinged back to the barracks, hiding him from the wrath of the upperclassmen: "Cooperate and Graduate" in action.

But there were those cadets who didn't play the cooperate game; they were competing in an individual sport, not a team sport. They wanted to look good, at all costs. A Tac had to be perceptive to catch it. These guys always impress their superiors. It's their peers whom they stab in the back. They're at West Point; they're at Harvard; they're at McDonald's flipping burgers.

Our tac, Major Lowe (behind his back, we called him "Hank"), became synonymous with "Management By Objectives" or "MBOs." MBOs were a '70s approach to business that Hank carried over to his cadets. We had to set MBOs—lovingly referred to as Mumbos— in everything from two-mile run times to physics grades.

MBO Lowe spent a lot of time wandering the halls of the barracks, checking on our Mumbo accomplishments and trying to keep us out of trouble. He was not the kind of guy who bet on the under-dog. To him, the underdog was merely one swift kick away from being booted out of West Point. The best way to get on Hank's good side was to under-set your Mumbos. Linda and I didn't figure out until it was too late that setting a Mumbo for an A in Electrical Engineering was like betting on the Red Sox before Ortiz. Not going to happen and only going to disappoint everyone concerned, especially Hank.

Every cadet in the company sat down in Hank's office at the beginning of the school year to discuss our Objectives and again in the spring, to see if we'd met them and to discuss summer training options. When I met with Major Lowe, I felt a little bad about being so non-Hooah.

"What about Airborne School, Cadet O'Sullivan?"

I paused. There wasn't one bone in my body that wanted anything to do with jumping out of airplanes. But I wasn't sure how to respond. I wanted to do the right things; I followed all the rules, shined my belt buckles and shoes. I knew I *should* have wanted to be Airborne, to earn this badge to wear on my uniform, to be a good hooah cadet. I didn't want to let the Tac down and I didn't want to confess to him that Buckner was not fun, sweating in the sand pits getting mauled in hand-to-hand combat, low-crawling up a hill to assault an objective with that steel pot bashing into my nose every time I jerked my head down, one obstacle course after another, each one higher than the last—or so it seemed to me. I was afraid of heights, was actually scared to death of them, didn't do roller coasters—still—but had managed to psyche myself through this stuff so far. How long would that last?

I couldn't lie. They were big on that at West Point.

"Sir, I really don't want to go to airborne school this summer. I didn't enjoy that part of Buckner and don't think I'll enjoy airborne school. If it's something I need to do in the Army, then I can try to go after graduation."

I was taken back with Hank's response. "Good. Let's send you to CTLT, then come back here to be a Beast squad leader."

Huh? This was almost too good to be true. Things like this didn't happen to me! "CTLT" stood for Cadet Troop Leader Training. For four weeks, cadets were assigned to units at Army posts all over the world to serve with platoons and get a taste of life in the real Army. Beast squad leader? I wasn't sure about that, hadn't even given it a thought. In the seventies, usually first classmen, rising senior cadets, were assigned to the Beast detail. I assumed that I'd be at Beast the next year, before my firstie year. Hank was smooth.

"CTLT will show you the real Army. You need to see what that's all about. You need to see that it's not going to be like Infantry week at Buckner for you every day. Then come back here for Beast. Most of the cadre will be firsties, but I have a few slots for cows. I'd like to put you in a leadership role at Beast and see how you do. If you do well, next summer, you'll be able to return to Beast in a different role or go out to Buckner in a leadership role."

This guy could have sold sand to the Saudis. I surmised that Hank wanted a female high-roller. Sad to say, I was about all he had. Though Linda was a good cadet, a rule-follower, she drove Hank nuts every semester. She was usually "D" (deficient; i.e., had a D or F) going into term-end exams, and though she passed every course, every semester, her last minute cramming sent Hank's blood pressure soaring. He eventually gave up on her. Teesa was too rambunctious and clearly not into the whole rule thing. There was talk that she was going to be moved to a different company so she could get a new start her junior year. Lori was smart and athletic, and would in fact earn a job at battalion-level despite her candor that made Patton look like Emily Post.

Liz, the sensitive, smart and caring city girl, had gotten in trouble. They'd been gunning for her. They were out to get her. A select number of Jerks in the Class of '79 took it upon themselves to try to catch Liz and her boyfriend, one of their own classmates, doing something they could get in trouble for doing. Every night, the Jerks entered their rooms, after taps, with flashlights. Finally, one night in the late spring of Liz's yearling year, they were caught: fully clothed, kissing on his bed. The offense, posted for corps-wide dissemination, as all offenses were (West Point's version of that loud speaker in my grammar school) was written up as "Engaging in acts of affection." If that doesn't leave room for conjecture! Liz, labeled as a slut, humiliated and shamed, was immediately moved to a different company. Walking across the area, with all her belongings in a laundry cart, male cadets shouted lewd remarks to her out the barracks window.

Can you imagine being in your 20s, kissing your boyfriend in his dorm room at a regular college, and *this* happening? One of the guys involved with this witch hunt later admitted that he doubted they would have cared if their classmate had been going out with a girl from Ladycliff (the women's college off post, since closed down), but since their classmate was going out with a female cadet, he was asking for trouble. The bottom line with PDA (Public Displays of Affection) was if we females got caught doing anything by anyone who cared (and that was key—a lot of guys didn't give a hoot or holler who was doing what with whom, would walk in and walk out, and never say a word to a soul), then our reputation was shot, with a double-barreled shot gun. That shot-gun left scars on Liz for years.

By the process of elimination, I was Hank's only possible female high roller. He had visions of me "out of the company" firstie year, in a leadership position on a staff somewhere, battalion, regiment or brigade. All would depend upon my first real leadership experience as a beast squad leader. And what did I do?

I fell in love.

My summer itinerary meant no leave, no vacation at all, but "Boring" is my middle name and I had no overwhelming desire to stand like an under-watered, potted plant at happy hour at the Cape again. I was excited about my summer. After graduation for the Class of '79, I flew to Frankfurt, West Germany where a red-faced, beefy soldier with watery eyes waited with a dirty green van to drive me to the Military Intelligence Company at Wurzburg in the 3rd Infantry Division. I'd been on that Air Force plane to Ft. Knox and then the F-2 Girls Trip to Florida, but flying to Europe, the bill on Uncle Sam, on a huge airplane, with movies, was a milestone in my life. I felt like Elly Mae hitting Beverly Hills.

The only Army post I'd ever seen, except for the tank training at Ft. Knox, was West Point, red brick homes, manicured lawns, protective chapels guarding the hillsides, striking officers sporting Ranger tabs and Combat Infantry Badges, their green jackets stacked with rows of colored medals. When I walked down the street of the run-down kaserne in Wurtzburg, I was stunned. Paint peeled from the buildings, dirt reeked from their WW II seams. The barracks reminded me of the "projects" back home in Roxbury, beat-up, run-down buildings, minus only the drug dealers in their cars with shiny, silver hub caps. *What's wrong with this picture?* The motor pools looked tired and greasy, overworked and underpaid. The off-duty soldiers bopped down the street in front of the worn building marked "Post Theatre" with boom boxes the size of small tanks on their shoulders. Is this the Army?

I needed Cadet Troop Leader Training. I needed it badly. I craved information about the real Army. I knew nothing and was forming a distorted image based upon squared away male officers, zero female officers, beautiful architecture, and eating the head off live chickens. I needed some reality. I sure got it in Wurzburg.

As a kid, I watched a TV show called F-Troop, a spoof on the old cavalry units that fought the Indians in the 1800s. Sadly, F-Troop, along with McHale's Navy, an equally goofy show about the Navy during WW II, was my only real media exposure to the military. In the opening scene of every F-Troop episode, the bungling, concerned Wilton Parmenter, reports to his commanding officer, tripping over a rug and falling splat on his face. Call me Wilton.

I was scared and nervous when I reported to the company commander of the Military Intelligence Company I was assigned to. I wanted to impress this Captain, a non-West Pointer; I wanted him to give me a real job. We heard about the cadets who actually got to be platoon leaders, the coveted job that all graduates hope for after graduation. We also heard about the cadets who did nothing in CTLT but follow their platoon leader around for four weeks. I wanted to be fully engaged. This initial meeting, I realized, was critical.

I tripped. Not over a rug, but over a step that led down into his small cave of an office in the basement of the dilapidated building which housed the MI company. It was a big trip. A Wilton Parmenter trip. A trip which prompted me to immediately pop off with, "I can't believe I did that. Just like on F-Troop!" before I came to attention and reported, "Sir, Cadet O'Sullivan reports."

Captain Young, fortunately, laughed and told me he watched F-Troop, too.

I got a platoon anyway. He didn't have a choice, actually. His platoon leader was going on leave and I was all he had. I'd be the acting platoon leader for the Collection and Jamming Platoon, a group of thirty-eight soldiers who maintained and operated equipment that intercepted and jammed enemy communications. The soldiers were sullen, glum, and miserable, and the equipment was broken. I was so excited.

For about a day. The guys were all over me. Not in a sexual way. They learned that when I went back to West Point on the first day of my cow year, I would incur, along with the rest of my classmates, an "obligation." The first day of cow year means "Commitment." Back then, we just showed up for our first class, understanding that if we quit or were kicked out from that day on, we owed time and money to the Army. (Today, the cows take an oath, and make it official.) Upon graduation, we served five years on active duty. If we were booted or failed out before graduation, we owed time as an enlisted soldier. So Specialist Davies and Specialist Weathers, both of whom had college degrees and were German linguists, spent their every waking moment arguing and insisting that I quit, now, no, yesterday, while I could. They were not happy soldiers. The pay, they told me, was awful. The hours, they whined, were worse. The working conditions were the pits. They were linguists and they spent their days in the motor pool under jeeps, firing up generators, scrounging parts, doing paperwork. They were only trying to help me out, they insisted. This man's army was the last place on earth I'd want to be.

This was 1979. There were still remnants of the "FTA" ("F*** The Army") sentiment, the post-Viet Nam bitterness had soaked into the bones of the Army ranks and morale was low. If a soldier was told that they'd be in the field over the weekend, if an inspection of the barracks was scheduled for after duty hours, if morning PT runs got longer and harder, if the food in the mess hall tasted like plastic, the answer was "FTA."

I was so disappointed. Davies and Weather were right; that surprised and saddened me. They worked long hours, were in the field more than not, did not keep up with their language skills and counted down the days until their enlistments were up. The days, I thought. Even in the real Army. It wasn't anything like I thought it would be like out there.

Sometimes, the weirdest things create allegiances. Or maybe the allegiance is already there, but the weirdest things bring it up to the surface. Like at West Point. I felt an allegiance to that institution and a responsibility to make it look good, to show the world that it did the right thing by letting women in: See me! I'm doing a good job, so it was the right thing!

And now the same thing in the Army. I felt an allegiance to the Army and a responsibility to do a good job, though I seem to have claimed it as my profession before I'd even met it. I wondered if I maybe just didn't give things enough thought. Maybe if I'd gone to U. Mass and was swept into a Hari Krishna movement, I'd be wearing a robe and chanting in Boston Common. But I hadn't. I was swept up by Duty, Honor, Country. I believed in it. And so, there I was in a motor pool in Wurzburg, defending my chosen profession. No rationale, but a whole lot of feeling.

It may have been the old wanna-be nun kicking in. I wanted to be a nun to help other people. The Army of the late '70s filled its ranks with soldiers like Davies and Weathers, unhappy, but talented people, and I was an idealist who thought I could make a difference, make a mark on the soldiers. I still believe that's what it's all about.

CTLT was an eye-opener. West Point, I learned, sadly, was not the Army. The platoon leader who sponsored me, an easy-going, smart, likable West Pointer, whose job was to sponsor and guide me, was having an affair with an enlisted soldier. She wasn't in the same unit, but this was still against all the rules. All of his soldiers knew about the girlfriend. They all liked her. I did, too. She had cancer. I didn't know how sick she was; I couldn't ask. I saw the rules being disobeyed by a good officer and I empathized with him for breaking them. What was the right answer? Why didn't they teach us about this stuff in Military Science class, instead of making us memorize the Principles of War? And what about the company commander? He was a twit! He didn't know it, but all the soldiers did. The soldiers, as a matter of fact, knew everything about everything, or thought they did anyway. If they weren't in the motor pool, or sometimes even if they were, they were drunk or high. There weren't many females out there in the Army. There were four female soldiers in my platoon. There were no female officers in the company. People were looking at me: the "female West Pointer." I didn't want to let them down, but I wasn't going to change either. I didn't have to. The platoon did what they needed to do without me having to be bitchy. They felt sorry for me, but when they said good-bye, I was convinced that I'd be OK with my personality out there in the leadership world. I still didn't know which end was up. But I thought I did. That was the frightening part.

Since I had no leave, I flew directly from Frankfurt to JFK Airport in New York, then was supposed to find the shuttle bus that was supposed to be sitting somewhere in the parking lot waiting to bring cadets to West Point, then was supposed to get back, sign in, unpack and begin training the next day to learn how to be a beast squad leader. I stood in line in Frankfurt with my sky blue suitcase, thinking how easy it was to pick a cadet out in a crowd. It was the hair—or lack of it, that is. There was a cadet right in front of me, no hair and clothes out of the Cadet Store, smiling wide and brimming with conversation he wanted to share. Not my favorite kind of person, but I had no place to go; couldn't even go to the bathroom or I'd lose my place in line, so I found myself telling him where I'd been, where I was going, where I was from, and by the time we reached the ticket counter, this new best friend, Steve, knew more about me than my mother. He wasn't shy. He asked if I wanted to sit next to him on the plane and though I was a little nervous about where this was going, I was too wimpy to say No, so we ended up sitting together for the eight-hour flight.

Once he mentioned his girlfriend in New Jersey, I was more comfortable with the conversation. I enjoyed male friendships, but the romance dimension always ruined it. Besides, I was still writing to Andrew, my Buckner platoon leader, the suave savior in the Orlando nightclub. We were still going out, I thought; I was changing him to a one-woman man, and I was not looking for a new romance. Steve talked a lot about his New Jersey girlfriend; I was safe.

"Come by and get me and we'll go for a run tonight," he'd said as he left me at the airport. Susan was meeting him and driving him up to West Point.

"Sure," I'd said. I liked running with other people, chatting while we ran, though I worried my pace would slow people down. No problems with the pace, he assured me, just want to do some junk miles to lose some schnitzel calories.

After dinner that night, unpacked and moved in to my new barracks room, jet-lagged and lonely, I thought a run would help my morale. I took off my white over grey uniform, hung it up in the wardrobe, and changed into gym alpha and running shoes, left my room and wandered down the hallways reading nametags on the doors. I saw his last name "Sosland" and knocked on the closed door—twice, like a good cadet. I always knocked twice like a good cadet, but rarely heard anything after I knocked. I usually just walked in, assuming they had said "Enter." Sitting on a bed, with no shirt on, playing a guitar was a guy, not Steve from the airplane. He stopped playing and looked up at me.

"Um, is this Steve Sosland's room?"

"Yeah. He's just at the latrine. He should be right back." The guy just kept looking. I guess, what was he supposed to do, go back to "Stairway to Heaven." I wasn't into music. Guys played hockey where I was from, not musical instruments.

"Um. OK." *Now what do I do*, I'm thinking.

The guitar is still in his lap. *Should I go outside and wait?* He interrupts my thoughts. Looking at my name on my gym uniform shirt (on any other female cadet, he'd be seeing breasts, but on me, it was just my name.), he says, "O'Sullivan, eh? My name used to be O'Dwyer, but we dropped the O."

"Oh," I respond. *What a weird guy*, I think.

That night, after I ran with Steve, showered and dropped onto my bed, I thought about what I was doing. My limbs felt crushed with loneliness. Everything was heavy—except for thoughts of self-pity that flew teasing and haunting. None of my classmates were here. Except for my roommate, all the other squad leaders and cadre members were firsties. And my roommate was Karen, the girl from Buckner who still, I'll admit it, intimidated me. No leave, no friends, and what about this boyfriend of mine. The longer I went without seeing that smile, the easier it was to forget about it. But if I were really changing him, how could I dump him? But was I really changing him? I was too tired to think about it. The only note I had in my positive column was this friendship with Steve Sosland. I was glad that I ended up behind him in line in Frankfurt.

Most of the cadre in my beast company were from F-2, and the computer that assigned the Class of 1980, back in their plebe year, to Company F-2 had a heck of a sense of humor. Think personalities of Seinfeld, zaniness of Austin Powers, military decorum of M*A*S*H. Toss like a fruit salad together in one company, in one class, living in one hallway, driving one tactical officer crazy. An interesting lot, they all shared one common denominator: they just wanted to have fun. You don't see "Fun" as a heading in the

West Point admissions information.

They simply refused to take anything, including the rules, too seriously. A few of them were bothered by the women in their class, the same old "I'm doing what they're doing, why are they on the cover of the *New York Times Magazine* for doing it?" The males in the Class of '80 who expressed concern that women were receiving publicity for doing the same thing as the men (which, of course, was very true), came across as the third child, the jealous, insecure one who gets left home a lot by mistake; the mother doesn't realize he's missing until she's unloading the beach chairs and counts kids.

I don't think it was jealousy they felt, as much as a feeling that these women watered down the machismo of their experience. It can't be as tough and as hard as everyone at home thinks it is if *chicks* are doing it. But, since this was the Class of '80 in F-2, they weren't into that whole machismo thing. That tough, hooah mentality belonged in First Regiment. The Zoo just wanted to have fun. So, despite a few of the guys being disappointed in the co-ed status West Point had achieved with their class, most of them had enough worries of their own—not getting caught drinking in the barracks, trying to pass physics, trying to accomplish at least one Mumbo and keep Hank off their backs—and didn't have the time or the energy to worry about the whole female thing.

They adopted me. They allowed me to join their group, treated me like a little sister, brought me with them to the Yankees game on our free Saturday night before the detail started. Steve Sosland and his roommate, the lanky guitar-playing guy, also named Steve, hung out with the clique and we spent most of our training laughing. I remained a rule-follower; they just accepted that in me.

I began running every night with Steve Sosland, but then he invited his roommate to join us, who turned out to be sort of funny, and then the first Steve somehow stopped showing and it was just the tall Steve and me running every night. He made me laugh and even more important, he thought I was funny. *I* always thought *I* was funny but not everyone agreed. Even Josie, who is not even a little bit funny, had written under my yearbook picture in high school, SHAT (Slightly Humorous At Times), which sort of offended me because I thought it could have said HAT, or at least UHAT (Usually).

There wasn't a skinny bone in my body that wanted anything romantic to do with this guy. He was too tall for me, about a foot taller, and he wasn't my type, much too laid back and not serious enough. He did have a few positives: he was Catholic, that was good, and he called his mother, which I liked. He was becoming a good friend quickly, and it usually takes me about a year to open up to people, so I must have been really lonely or desperate for company. I knew that once our training was complete, once the detail changed and we were squad leaders, we'd have no time for socializing.

The ultimate leadership challenge, I thought when I left active-duty and became one, is being an Army wife; but in 1979, I was convinced that it was being a Beast squad leader. I was worried. It would have been easier, I thought, to have been first detail when the new cadets are very dumb and know nothing else. New cadets usually think their first detail squad leader is God. Mine was. Now, though, new cadets will be comparing me to the first detail squad leader, and I know my second detail squad leader was nowhere near God, not even close. Did my squad like their first squad leader? Had they learned anything? Are they squared away? Did I have any females?

I never learned whether or not they liked their first squad leader—not very professional to ask and a dead give-away that I'm a tad insecure. Three of them were Prepsters and squared away, though one, a tall, confident kid, verged on belligerent, and when he whistled at me—a cat call! In the barracks!—as I returned from the shower to my room in my bathrobe, I was beside myself, couldn't even face him, had the platoon leader go yell at him and then avoided eye contact for a good week. The others were average, good kids, trying hard, getting by. And females, did I ever have them. Five! How could they give me five females? I didn't get it. Females at West Point were like animals on Noah's Ark; they came in twos. Two per squad was the norm. But FIVE? And who was I supposed to ask "WHY FIVE?" I wanted to think it was because "they" thought I would provide outstanding leadership and mentoring to these female new cadets, but since the first detail squad leader was a male, that theory was hogwash. I just plumb got five females.

There were two problems with having females in my squad. First, females meant instant visibility. I wanted to be unseen. Second, I cut the females no slack. I was not blessed with an abundance of sympathy. The other day, my son hurt himself. "Mom, I'm bleeding," he tells me. In a New York second, I reply, "Wash it off; don't get it on the carpet." He asked me if I wanted to see the wound, *did I care at all*? If a female cadet fell out of a run because she had her period and felt lousy, my gut reaction, I'm not proud to say, was *Take Your Period to Boston College.*

Of course, this was easy for me to say because I had none. None! Not the entire four years! During that lecture in Beast, when the Dragon Lady talked to us about periods, she mentioned amenorrhea but I wasn't really listening. Besides, *why* I didn't get periods didn't matter to me. Lack of body fat? Not eating enough vegetables? Who cares? Life is easier without periods at West

Point; that's a fact, Jack. My mother made me go to a doctor over summer break before my yearling year. They checked my pituitary gland and said everything was OK; they told me to see a specialist if I wanted to get pregnant. I was so lucky to not have periods during Buckner. A friend had hers on Recondo, changing a tampon in the woods on a night patrol, sticky and dirty, M-16 leaning against a tree, hoping the ambush waited five more minutes. I couldn't even imagine it.

I knew I was hard on female cadets, but didn't think I was harder on them than I was on male cadets. I expected them to blend in, to know the rules, look sharp in their uniforms, not fall out of runs, not fall out of road marches. The females in my squad were good cadets. Calvert was about four feet tall, built like a little monkey and could do one-armed push-ups, which was very impressive. Gray was a normal girl who tried hard in everything and I liked that. Barone was tough, an athlete, focused, dedicated. (Twenty-five years later, Lieutenant Colonel Barone would be the commander of Beast Barracks for our oldest son in the Class of 2009!) And Fogle was a character. She was from Harlem and one evening after dinner, another squad leader came up to me and said, "Fogle had gum."

"OK," I said, "I'll talk to her." Gum was a no-no. New cadets weren't supposed to have gum, never mind be chewing it in public and getting caught.

The squad leader had a funny look on his face. "There's more."

"Huh?"

He smiled then. "I told her to get rid of it and she took it out of her mouth and put it behind her ear, then kept walking down the hall."

"Her EAR?"

I called Fogle out into the hallway and asked her to explain. She very seriously told me she didn't want to waste the gum, hence, the placement behind her ear, like she had done this often. Maybe the squad leaders were learning more than the new cadets, I thought. That wad of bazooka behind the ear taught me that not everyone was brought up in Braintree, Massachusetts; not everyone thought the way my mother and Aunt Rita did.

The females turned out to be a non-issue. They blended in, except on one road march when the little one, Calvert, decided to hyper-ventilate. I ran up to where she was panting. The other new cadets marched by us on the hill, one by one, slowly, worried. I was worried, too. I grabbed her rucksack off her back and thought *Now what?* My roommate's squad was coming up the hill and Karen came over to help. She thought to take the steel pot and cover her face, for lack of a paper bag. Calvert's breathing eventually slowed down, I was impressed with Karen's cool hand, and was overwhelmed with the awesome responsibility I had for these "kids." Leadership humbled me. It scared me, too.

The rumor mill said that I had the number one football recruit in my squad. I never asked if that was true and I didn't know anything about football so, to me, Benson was just another new cadet, a really big one. He was 6'6" and built like a brick house. In formation, I eye-balled him about at belt buckle level. He was quiet, not a trouble-maker, but not eating it up either. I didn't think he was happy, most new cadets aren't, but I was surprised when he told me he wanted to quit. I talked to him. He knew nothing about West Point or the Army. He wanted to play football. Period. In Texas. End of discussion.

I wrote a letter to his parents. I told them that he gave West Point his best effort, that he made this decision with much thought, that West Point was not for everyone and if their son didn't want to be in the Army, then perhaps this decision was the right one for him. I never heard back from them. I wondered if I'd said something wrong, if they were disappointed in their son, if they cared.

We lost Benson but we gained, peculiarly, Huerra. New cadets start on R-Day, not a week into second detail. Huerra, a little guy from California, reported on R-Day with his classmates, but quit right before change of detail, went back home to California, woke up the next morning and said I Made a Big Mistake. For some reason, West Point said You May Come Back, and for some reason, they put him in my squad. I couldn't think that it was because I was such a little Patton; it was probably just because we'd lost the football player. The cadet counselor, a psychologist, a friendly, long-haired, not typically military guy, Lieutenant Colonel Wilson, took me aside to talk to me about Huerra. This would pose leadership problems for me, he realized. The other new cadets might not accept him; he'd missed so much of what they had endured. He'd slept a full day! They would kill for sleep, even for an accident-induced coma!

We were standing behind the formation, which was marching into the mess hall. I'm hot, I thought. I'm tired. Why did I get this guy?

We judged—as only young twenty-year-olds who know everything can judge—that officers were assigned to "Non-Kill The Enemy" roles, (like LTC Wilson, the psychologist) because they lacked hooah. In reality, some had more leadership skills than I'd develop in my lifetime. LTC Wilson told me, "You got Huerra because you can handle this." He continued, "You'll be firm but fair. You'll treat him like everyone else, like he's been here all along, but you'll see that he gets the training he missed."

I thought of LTC Wilson's advice fifteen years later when we adopted an eighteen-month-old child from Paraguay and threw her into a squad of three boys.

"To lead the people, walk behind them."

—Lao Tzu

Green or bronzed men, Eisenhower, Patton, MacArthur, hulking, almost paternal, daring us to be half of what they were, throw their shadows of leadership on the grasses of the plain. And cows find a way to walk all the way around and avoid being caught in these shadows. Cows are leadership morons, who were supposed to have tried leadership on for size as team leaders during yearling year, but found it just didn't fit. It was too tight and physics was too demanding to take the time to loosen it up, or it was too loose and apathy overruled and who really gives a hoot or holler. Beast squad leaders who are cows (and today, that's all of them) are still finding themselves. Too friendly, jokey and low-key, or too hard-core, rigid and unyielding, cows haven't been around long enough to develop a mix of both styles; some don't figure it out for years.

I was Miss Straight as an Arrow. My mother wrote me a letter every Sunday night and in one that arrived in early August, she told me to look up a new cadet from Braintree. A girl. Her father worked with my dad for New England Tel and Tel, and his daughter had graduated from high school the same year as I had, although she'd gone to Braintree High, the public school. After graduation, when I left for West Point, Mary Ann left for Smith College. She'd been there for two years and was now a new cadet. I was amazed. Who would go to Smith for two years and then go to West Point?

I found out which company Mary Ann was in, but hesitated. I didn't want her to get any grief for having an upperclassman seek her out (*So do you think you're something special, New Cadet? You think maybe you can get away with something because you know an upperclassman?*). But, harder to admit, I didn't want to ruin my rep. I didn't want to be seen by the other upperclassmen as a female looking out for a female. I didn't want to be seen as someone who shows favoritism. It was my mother, again, saying: *What would the neighbors think?*

I did find Mary Ann. I wondered what she recalled of our experiences and so I called her, and talked to her for the first time in twenty-five years. She married a classmate, has two children and a Masters in English; she's balanced, happy and wise. I babbled my apologies, how badly I feel, how I should have mentored her, guided her, how sorry I was that I was in my own little bubble. No, she replied, instead of saying how distant and aloof I was, she phrased it like this, "You told me to call you if I needed anything, but I knew that would infringe upon the professional relationship you wanted to have with underclassmen."

We talked about sexual harassment and she said, yes, she experienced it. Why did she, I wondered, while I endured such minimal harassment? She didn't hesitate. She laughed and said,

"I had boobs."

I never thought about the fact that being boob-less probably helped me endure four years at West Point with little sexual harassment. Of course! Nothing bounces when I run. Nothing sticks out in my uniform. No problems with adjusting the load bearing equipment during the military training or the nametag on my class uniform. If I'd had a penis and had to shave in the morning, I'd have fit right in.

> "I never could get the cadet dating thing.
> It seemed like driving with the
> parking brake on. Why bother?"
>
> — Class of '81 male classmate, F-2

I couldn't believe it. That very intense feeling of No Romantic Interest Whatsoever in that tall guy with the guitar was weakening before my very brown eyes. What was this all about? Had I no control over these feelings? I didn't like this change one bit. Wasn't I going out with Andrew? I hadn't heard from him in a few weeks, but I thought we were still going out. Wasn't I changing him?

Towards the end of Beast, before our march out to Lake Frederick, we got a good deal, a Saturday night pass, and one of the F-2 guys, Stuban (why do males call each other by their last names?) invited us to his house in Connecticut for a cook-out. I drove with Steve—I had to. I had no car, he did, and he asked me. He had a used Toyota Celica, which impressed me. I was amazed at the cadets who used their car loans—at the time, it was $5,000 at 3% interest—on a gas-guzzling, neon-colored, big-wheeled hot rod, so I admired his practical approach to car buying (only to learn later that he blew his loan on a trip to Bermuda).

And then came some regular girls. Female cadets normally had a jealousy issue towards "regular" females who had long hair and real tans and didn't spend their summer living in the barracks. All of a sudden, how it happened I don't know. In the backyard, wavy blond hair and short shorts and bubbly, like they stepped off a double-mint commercial, were two girls, all over Steve. First off, what's this all about, I wanted to know. He's not that good looking! Go hang all over someone else! What really bugged me though was *Why was this bugging me?* We're only friends! Let him go for these dizzy, eyelash-batting, arm holding broads!

I was furious at myself for being jealous. This was not in the plan. It would make my life way too confusing. I was falling fast for this guy and what about Andrew, whom I was personally converting into a one-woman man? As it turned out, I was doing about as much conversion as a mute Mormon. We were back at West Point, after the cookout with the teeny-bopper Hooters, walking down the steps of the mess hall, surrounded by Beanheads, when a friend mentioned in passing that he'd seen my Andrew over the weekend. Jim told me that he saw him over Richardson's house; he was going out with Richardson's drop-dead-gorgeous sister, did I know that?

It was a relief. OK, it was actually a tremendous blow to my ego, but my ego had taken so many blows since R-Day, it had become pretty resilient. If I'd been head over heels in love with this Romeo, it would have hurt more. It was like someone whammed me over a head with a frying pan full of all the comments Linda and my parents had made since Spring break.

I told my friend Steve about the end to my quasi-romance. Did I see relief or was he just trying to give a comforting face? I knew this meant that we could be more than friends, but I wasn't sure how much more either of us wanted. I was still not keen about the idea of going out with a cadet. It did nothing for my very straight reputation. They actually said we women came to West Point to find a husband. What a crock that was. Like we were more marketable here? Did that steel pot and weapon make us desirable women, capable of dealing with door-to-door salesman and household intruders? Wouldn't I be more likely to find a man at a place I could wear regular clothes and mascara, like U. Mass? I just wanted to be a good cadet, wanted to study, run, and shine my shoes without someone interfering.

Steve was fine with us being only friends; he must have ascertained by this point that he wasn't going to get anything out of me, and he seemed OK with it. I figured if he wanted romance, he'd have gone for someone with a body anyway. With looks like mine, you knew guys didn't go out with you for being a Baywatch look alike. He was the kind of guy who was into minimal stress in his life and if a romance were to interrupt a nap, he'd have to do some serious thinking and prioritizing.

✦ ✦ ✦ ✦

I like to be liked.

I wanted my Beast squad to like me but I realized, from reading the books that those behavioral science teachers made us read, from listening to endless leadership lectures; this might not happen.

It was the last time we'd be together as a Beast squad. We were on the apron, in front of the barracks, bone weary, emotionally drained. We had road-marched fourteen miles back from Lake Frederick, had eaten our last meal together in the mess hall, and were about to go our separate ways. The Class of '83 would march off to their academic companies. I remembered the stress from my own experience and I felt for them.

I knew something was up. They came to attention on their own. One of the Prepsters seemed to be in charge. In unison, they all shouted The Ripper, one of the cheers they had been required to learn for their plebe knowledge. But they announced it as "The RIPPAH!" - the way I do, and as loud as their tired bodies would allow, with my Boston accent, heavily exaggerated, they screamed:

"A—Ahhhhhh- M-Y, T- E-A-M,

A—Ahhhhhhh- M-Y, T-E-A-M,

Ahhhhhhh—ME, TEAM FIGHT!"

One of those poignant leadership moments, my eyes welled up. I'm cold as ice most of the time, but when something twangs on a weak spot, I'm an emotional slob. I shook their hands good bye and my squad left to begin their plebe year. I watched them all go, hoped I'd made a mark on them, then grabbed my gear and trudged through the area to Central Barracks, and up the five flights of stairs to F-2.

Gail marching back from Lake Frederick
with her squad, members of the Class of
1983. August 1983

eleven

Cow Year: Running Too Slow, Falling Too Fast

"When you do something, you should burn yourself up completely, like a good bonfire, leaving no trace of yourself."

—Shunryu Suzuka

I was still running, in my free time, whenever I could find an hour here or there. I was addicted. Meg, a classmate with whom I'd been in some classes, a bright, shy, petite blond, ran both cross country and track. She'd run in high school and she was good.

We were walking to class one morning and she asked me, "If you're going to run every day, why don't you try out for the team? You'd get out of parades if you were on the team."

She was honest with me. There were some new plebe recruits and there were some extraordinary yearlings. I'd never run competitively in my life and figured there was no way I'd make the team. Until I went to West Point, I shied away from things I was likely to do poorly in. But from R-Day on, I was more than likely to do poorly in most things, and was used to trying, only to fail and have to try again. Still, I surprised myself by showing up for those try-outs.

Women't Cross Country team before leaving for a meet. Fall 1979

I ran my heart out. I had no choice; that was about all I had. No innate talent, no form, no knowledge, no nothing—except sheer mental will and apparently an OK heart. I made the cross country team. Barely, but I was all right with that.

I loved practices. I hated meets. Practices were no stress, miles of chatting with good friends. Meets were competition, book-ended by dry heaving. Throwing up wouldn't have been that bad if I'd at least done well in the meet, but to throw up and still finish last is a real bummer. The team, no thanks to me, was good and we went to the National Championships in Florida. I vowed that meet on the sunny golf course in Tallahassee would be my last. True to my word, it was.

The coach was a nice guy, but didn't spend a lot of time talking me out of my decision. He didn't spend a lot of time talking to me at all. One comment he made to me has stayed with me for years. Watch what you say to people! It was after one grueling practice on the golf course, running intervals on hills, me just trying to keep up with someone, anyone, and not trying to throw up until practice was over.

We finished finally and he called me over. "I don't know how you even finish a meet with that form of yours." I think it was sort of a left-handed compliment. I waited for further guidance, but he didn't give it, nor did I ask. What should I look like? What should I do different? I just kept running, mind over matter, and hoped form and anything else I needed to know would eventually come to me. It didn't.

I threw up because I pushed myself beyond where I'd trained; I tried to keep up with with Meg, with Sue, a member of the Class of '80 who was hysterical, kind and talented; with Harlene, Amy, MaryAnn, Roberta and Sarah, whose friendship made all those miserable meets worth it. I pushed my body to limits I had no business being close to. I refused to admit that I couldn't keep up with my teammates. I didn't know how to compete with myself. I only knew how to compete with others.

If I'd known about self-competition, I would have saved myself from a lot of dry heaving. Beat yourself and if you beat anyone else in the process, be gracious. It's a good rule for life.

MBO Lowe was all over me cow year. He never said anything about my new tall friend. He did congratulate me on making the cross-country team; he thought this would push me into becoming more competitive and aggressive. I disappointed him.

In the fall, we took the two-mile run test for grade, down along the scenic Hudson and the sewerage plant. Hank showed up to run with the cows in F-2, a major in his mid-thirties, wearing his combat boots and his PT uniform. He found me as we lined up. He never said much to me, just looked down from behind his birth control glasses and quietly said, half smiling, "I'm going to run with you."

He kicked my skinny little ass. I couldn't let this old guy beat me. (This was before mastering that self-competition rule.) For a fleeting second, I had my name up on the records chart in the gym. Two Mile Run, Gail O'Sullivan. Women's best time: 13:06.

I always felt like I should have two asterisks next to it.

*Time due only to the efforts of Hank Lowe

*This girl was kicked off intramural volleyball!

(By the time they'd put the first asterisk up though, the record would be broken by one of those extraordinary yearlings.)

"It's much easier to turn a friendship
into love, than love into friendship."

—Proverb

When I wasn't paying attention, Steve and I switched gears from "Just Friends" to "Going Out." At least for a while, I figured. I had no expectations. I'd started the Septembers of both my plebe and yearling years with a boyfriend, but by the first quiz in math class, had managed to run them both off. Who knew what would happen with this one.

In 1979, dating between cadets was not yet defined. I'm not sure they've got the definition down now either. There are questions like: He went to

Grant Hall with her and they got ice cream, but he goes out with a girl back home. Is that dating? They went to the hockey game together, walked to the rink, sat together with the guys in his company. Is that dating? They left a company party, he was drunk, kissed her, she's smitten, wants to quit and marry him, but he's engaged to a colonel's daughter. Is that dating?

There was only one undisputable truth about dating a female cadet: It was not cool.

It was worse than going out with your sister. Female cadets weren't "real girls." They bussed real girls in from real colleges in real dresses for the dances. Honestly, they did. They finally stopped sending those yellow busses full of long haired honeys through the gates my firstie year, but by then, the damage was done. They'd convinced us we didn't count as real girls. It really didn't bug me as much as it should have. I never claimed to be a knock-out. I knew my mediocre looks had taken a hit on R-Day and were being whacked daily ever since. One of the guys I knew in high school even told someone "Gail had a decent butt in high school, but that's gone now." Ouch. (I figured my butt had just dissipated with everything else since R-Day.) Even my mother added to the misery when she gave all those prom dresses away. Maybe if I'd had my favorite, the long sleeveless peach silk dress with a hood, still hanging in my closet, I would have been able to think there was *some* femininity left in my life *somewhere*.

I felt bad for Steve. Dating a female cadet was a true sign of desperation. It didn't matter if the female cadet had just graced the cover of the *Sports Illustrated* swimsuit edition in her cadet issue bathing suit. (OK, SI wasn't calling, but there were some female cadets, if dressed in more fashionable garb with a better beautician, who *were* cute.) No matter how good looking she was, the general consensus was that the male cadet who asked her out just hit rock bottom in the dating barrel; going out with a female cadet was the ultimate in lowering your standards.

Steve got a lot of grief from his classmates; his rugby teammates were particularly ruthless. I'd talked him into running with me every morning at 0530. It was a Cadet Date. Still true today, male cadet running with female cadet equals a cadet date, a ca-date. It was the only time we could see each other alone and talk. In my on-going attempt to improve my running so I could hang with the cross country team, I ran every morning anyway. When Steve committed to run with me, he was saying "yes, I like you enough to forego an hour of sleep" and "yes, I'll take crap for dating you, a female cadet—though most of the corps is still sleeping at that ungodly hour anyway, so I should be safe."

He *should* have been safe. The very first morning we ran together, we turned the corner at Grant Hall out of the barracks onto Thayer Road and were hit head on by thirty members of the rugby team whose guffaws made me want to find a sewer hole to creep into. Steve didn't care. He didn't care what people thought of him. You had to be that way to go out with a female cadet. Male cadets who dated female cadets had either self-actualized or were just really weird.

Dating any female cadet was hard enough. Dating *me* was a puzzle, an art. Ignore me and I'm yours. Come too close and I back off. Mess with my time and I back off. Don't even think about PDA in the barracks. Don't even think about breaking a rule with me around. I was not a barrel of fun when I was *not* dating.

Fortunately, Steve didn't want to mess with my study time; he was too busy trying to set a cadet record for most consecutive nights going to the movies. As busy as I was studying, he was equally, if not more, occupied with napping and eating ice cream at Grant Hall. He played me right. Though he would have liked something to accommodate his hormonal desires, he allowed for my rule-following, nun-like behavior, in obvious hopes that his time would come on weekend passes.

The problem with cadet dating in those days was that the cadet you dated in the barracks was not necessarily the person you dated on weekends. You lived for weekend passes. Then you wore real clothes and eye make-up, smiled more, laughed more. Weekend passes, Christmas leaves, Thanksgiving passes, all gave but honeymoon snapshots of the cadet you were dating. You hardly know this person you saw for three weekends a semester, then you marry him after graduation—if not, you'll end up in Korea and he'll be at Bragg—and then you wake up and say, *Who is this person?* How can you really get to know someone you see for thirty minutes a day overrun by cadet life chaos, and three weekends a semester overrun by sex-starved hormones? The divorce rate for cadet marriages in the early 80s is steeper than that Recondo run hill.

> "What helped you get through West Point intact
> at that time when women were still so new?
> Probably meeting Steve, the hotshot
> upperclassman who was strumming his guitar, didn't hurt.
> You were an Abbott and Costello team who seemed
> to have very deep roots in family, in mission,
> in integrity, and in love for each other."
>
> —Carolyn McNally

I introduced Steve to the McNally's in September. It was as important to me that they like him as it was that my parents like him. They'd never met any of my boyfriends before. I wasn't sure what they'd think. Steve was so laid back and I almost felt bad that I didn't go out with a high roller, an over-achiever, a rule follower, like me. Although he didn't get in trouble, I assumed that was most likely because he didn't get caught. He switched sports more than he changed his underwear, traveling between them, like a bee zapping from flower to flower. He went from football to lacrosse to rugby to track, where Captain McNally was the Officer-in-charge, and Steve threw the javelin, when not napping in the high jump pit.

Captain McNally was my sponsor. Every cadet at West Point is assigned a sponsor, an officer or non-commissioned officer, who invites you to his or her home to give you a view of Army family life. After the initial visit, the sponsor and the cadet sometimes continue the relationship, sometimes not, depending upon personalities, and the time and effort the sponsor is willing to commit. Captain McNally and his wife, Carolyn, adopted me.

I'd never met a couple like them before. They had no children and Carolyn had a high speed job with the State of Connecticut, driving two hours a day one-way to work. My father drove almost forty-five minutes to Framingham and I thought that was a long commute. I was afraid to sit on their furniture. Where I grew up, furniture was either covered with plastic in the living room or covered with food stains in the den. On Robinson Avenue, the Monti's had the wooden cut-outs of the lady bending over her garden, the Lawrence's had an elephant-like plastic pink pig in the front bay window (Irish tradition says to put a pig in your parlor, but most people prefer small ceramic ones), and the Shell's had skeletons of old cars, up on racks, scattered throughout both front and back lawns. I'd never used a cloth napkin and we only had one fork per meal in my family. Helping Carolyn prepare one meal, chopping something green and long on the thick wooden cutting board, I had to ask, "What are these?"

She smiled, but had to think I was a trailer trash moron.

"Scallions and green onions. Haven't you seen them before?"

"If they don't come frozen, no…."

The McNally's gave me friendship and taught me many things about life. They wrote the book on accepting people for who they are. I didn't have to worry about them with Steve.

"Some cause happiness wherever
they go; others, whenever they go."

—Oscar Wilde

Except for my roommate, life was as good as it gets at West Point. I was running cross country, doing OK in classes, and falling in love. But a bad roommate can make life wretched. My luck had run out after two years with Linda, Liz, Lori and Teesa as roomies. First semester cow year, I lived with a unique character.

The Tac came to see me in my room at the end of Beast, before we marched out to Lake Frederick. I knew this was not a good thing. Tacs usually don't just visit. He started off with the dessert of course, telling me how great I was doing in Beast. I almost fell out of my chair when he told me that I was the number four female cadet in our class in PE. I wanted to scream and jump and fly that message on the Goodyear Blimp over my hometown, over all the people who thought I wouldn't be able to hang physically. I'm glad I didn't though. My PE rank dropped like a rock when we started taking electives, the fun courses like racquetball, tennis and golf, which required eye-hand coordination, a trait that must have been with breasts, skipping me and landing on the next baby in line at conception.

Hank eased me into the roommate situation. New girl coming to F-2, he said. She's had some problems getting along with people in her old company. You'll be her roommate first semester.

I'd seen her around, had been in some of her PE classes, but didn't know her. It's hard for me to be critical of people since I was a bit obsessive-compulsive myself, but everyone said that this girl had some issues. West Point draws the competitiveness out of people; most of us tried to do our best in everything, but when you were surrounded by talented people, you really had to believe what your mother used to say, "God gave everyone different talents, different gifts." At the beginning of my cow year, I was still searching for exactly what my gift was and I thought that perhaps I was short-changed in the gift line while in uterus. But I was OK with it.

Charlene was not. I had set my alarm for 5:30 a.m. for over a year to run a few miles before school. Linda, who had lettered in high school track, thought I was nuts. She had no trouble sleeping that extra half hour while her obsessed roommate hit the streets in the dark. Charlene couldn't do it.

She hated to run and routinely failed her two mile run tests. Yet, she told me she was going to run every morning, too. She got up, got dressed in her PE clothes, and we went our separate days. One morning, I returned to the room almost immediately to get some gloves, and caught her, back in the sack, in her PE clothes. She wanted me to think she was someone she wasn't, as if I cared. She had problems.

Most of the time, she was just miserable. Charlene sucked the energy out of a room. I spent most of my time at the library first semester cow year.

I flew to Philadelphia the day after Christmas my cow year, Steve's firstie year. We were going to spend some time at his family's then drive back to West Point together. We'd become closer, running in the mornings, eating optional breakfast together daily, talking at night before taps. We'd driven to his house for a weekend and to my house for a weekend and we'd talked about the future, but in vague, it's so far away, terms.

Two days after Christmas, on the couch alone watching TV late at night, he proposed. I wasn't surprised. I was stunned. My response was something very romantic, like "Shit!" Normally not a curser, he didn't take this as a good sign.

Where I'm from, the gifts you give are directly proportional to the years you have gone steady. At four months, we were looking at a sweater from a discount rack or maybe a cheap necklace from Bradlees. Where I'm from, you get engaged after a minimum of dating three years, with the preferred time frame being eight years (through both high school and college). A diamond? Granted, I couldn't really see the thing—and I had pretty good eyes—and he admitted he got it from Sosland whose father was a jeweler and it was a good deal, but it was still a diamond.

After my pop-off answer, I said YES without a trace of hesitation. Well, maybe just a little trace. I thought *this* guy was *the* guy, but I didn't have a good track record with absentee romances. Absence didn't make my heart grow fonder; I had proven to be an *out of sight, out of mind* kind of gal. I wanted to marry him, but who knew how I'd feel in a year, when he'd been gone for six months? I oozed with practicality. Our engagement would be eighteen months long. Anything could happen.

I didn't wear my ring at school and I didn't tell anyone except Linda and Meg that I was engaged. If dating a cadet opened the floodgates of gossip, imagine what being engaged did. Who needed the gossip?

When you live life in a bubble, you miss what's going on outside, in the real world. When Patty told me she was going to resign, I couldn't believe it. I knew she wasn't happy, but who was? Everyone complains at West Point; it's like breathing and sneezing, it just happens. Patty dated Dan, a guy in the Class of 1980. He was a squad leader in our Beast company, dark haired and daring, a nice guy, a free spirit. I assumed if things got serious that Patty would get engaged, graduate, and then marry him. It turns out Patty wasn't just outside my bubble; she was living on a whole different planet.

> "There was a fine line that all the
> women had to walk while at West Point—
> as if every male cadet and officer was
> looking at them and asking, 'Which are you?
> A dike or a whore? You must be one or
> the other or you wouldn't be here!'"
>
> —Patty Collins, ex-1981 USMA

That wasn't going on in my planet. On my planet, I felt only like I had to prove myself as capable, as qualified. No way could anyone think I was a whore. If you followed the rules, that just can't happen. I *was* worried that people might think I was a lesbian. It was mostly the hair. Haircuts from Big Ed were dyke-like. There wasn't anything we could do about it. We didn't have the option of growing our hair and looking like Farrah Fawcett on weekends. We had butch hair cuts seven days a week. I'd never worn make up in high school, maybe a touch of mascara for the prom with a bit of lip gloss, not much of a make-up queen. I preferred jeans and sneakers to skirts and heels. I fit many of the typical lesbian characteristics and worried that people thought I might be one, but what can you do. Most nights I wasn't getting enough sleep as it was and I wasn't going to lose sleep over the possibility of me looking dyke-like.

There were certainly some lesbians at West Point. The tough, athletic, no-nonsense, no frills personality that fit so well with the machismo atmosphere at West Point is the classic stereotype of a lesbian. I wondered if some of the girls who showed up on R-Day didn't really know which team they played on, and when it came to pick a side, they opted to go with the more friendly side. Of my seven roommates over the course of four years, two were lesbians, though I didn't know it at the time.

Lesbian stories were rampant. The corps labeled the entire women's basketball team as gay. The rumors flew: Away games were wild lesbian orgies; the female coach encouraged togetherness during Sunday afternoon socials at her house. This was all outside my bubble. I just didn't care. The biggest hullabaloo was a result of "innocent" star gazing from a telescope borrowed from the Astronomy Club by some studious First class cadets. It seems that their telescope inadvertently caught notice of two women in Pershing barracks. This was before shades. (Now all cadet rooms have shades.)

Cadets share and these budding astronomers made some quick phone calls from their room in Eisenhower Barracks to their friends throughout the corps. Soon the line of would-be star gazers snaked down the hall, with anxious, excited cadets who had a great excuse to not do their Engineering project, and who wanted to grab a quick glimpse of this porn flick. A cadet on brigade staff who happened to be in the hallway at the time took a peek and the rest is history. The two girls were both gone in three days.

In the Spring of cow year, we sat down one on one with the Tac again to discuss summer training. This summer, I wanted some leave. I was in love. And love screws your priorities up. Big time. Love means that your world is suddenly consumed only with the person with whom you are in love and you can't think about anyone except him/her. In retrospect, it is actually pathetic and very embarrassing. If you read the letters that you wrote when you were in Love twenty-five years later, you may become violently ill. Love grows from Serious Like, as mine did, without any planning. It just happens, like gray hair and knee wrinkles, without your blessing. Love is a temporary state, thank goodness, because long periods of Love are in fact dangerous. You can forget to eat, to sleep, to call your mother. Fortunately, and this occurs almost immediately after the "I Do's", Love fades to a more livable state, a lower-case l, where love is Of course I love you, but I'm really tired and let's just hold hands while we fall happily asleep beside each other. I just don't need anything more than that! Before you know it, you've eaten an entire bucket of drumsticks from KFC and are wearing a lime green muumuu around the house. You try to save a buck by looking in the desk drawer for the Anniversary card you gave him last year. Heck, he won't read it anyway, especially if you give it to him when "SportsCenter" is on.

I digress.

Towards the end of my cow year, I was in deep Love. That organized, squared away cadet was shifting priorities. I wanted to spend time with

Steve before he headed to his Infantry Basic Course at Ft. Benning, Georgia. The Tac agreed. I would be the S-4, the staff member in charge of logistics, for the second detail of Beast.

If we were barefoot and pregnant, it would have been the classic female role. Linda and I both played S-4 that summer; she was at Buckner and I was at Beast. We were the laundry and mess hall mamas. I was relieved to have been put in a staff position. I knew I was better at staff work than leadership. I'd be better at pro football than leadership. I was just glad that I would get the leave time I wanted. Plus, Hank, the ultimate salesman, assured me that this job was important and I would do well in it. I still just wanted to do well at something. I didn't want to stumble and fall anymore. I'd done that enough. Give me something that I could be good at!

Steve and Gail at Steve's graduation hop. May 1980

twelve

Last West Point Summer:
Logistics and Love

Picture this. A week at the beach in New Jersey together, holding hands in the Toyota Celica, heading south on I-95 toward Ft. Benning, Georgia, listening to Kool and The Gang, sipping from the same soda. You're sky high about life and you don't think about when that balloon will eventually pop and when it does, it's not pretty. You're at the airport and it doesn't pop; it explodes. Sobbing convulsively—me! The girl who didn't even cry when Big Ed took her hair off with a machete. On the plane, the elderly woman next me, leans over, her chins (and she has more than a Chinese phone book), hitting the arm rest, and says kindly, "First time away from home, honey?" I look about twelve and she must figure I'm going to Girl Scout camp. I show her my engagement ring, which I wear for good now. The diamond is hard enough to see without cataracts, but she nods politely. I just kept crying. Never did I imagine love would be so hard.

Beast hit me like a ton of bricks. I had no idea that S-4 meant getting the barracks ready, beds, linens, pillows, getting the meals lined up at the mess hall, making sure our laundry was going to be picked up, and there's no toilet paper in the latrine on the fourth floor! Fortunately, two kind and competent officers, Major Kahara and Captain Kettler, mentored, guided and laughed with me. I would have followed either of them anywhere. They were the

kind of leader I hoped to be someday. Firm but fair, compassionate, hard working, but with a sense of humor that said OK, this is important, but not important
enough for me to rant and rave and go ballistic about.

"I'm just a person trapped inside a woman's body."

—Elaine Boosler

The cadets on the regimental staff were eleven great guys. But the hard
part of working with a bunch of really competent people is that it's easy for
a dummy to feel incompetent. I was the only female. All of them were over-
achievers, really smart, hard working, a tad anal and extremely conscientious. Honestly, except for the really smart bit, that was me, too. I knew they
danced circles around me academically and intellectually, and I struggled to
keep up. The first few days, when I didn't know anything, if I was caught un-
prepared by a question at a briefing—"what is the plan for signing over the
red sashes from first detail to second detail?"—I spazzed. Spazzing is a combination of sputtering and awkwardness, seen often in people who have negative IQ scores. When I spazzed, I thought the other guys on the staff, the
squared away up and coming "high rollers", were looking at me like I was a
token. I was afraid that they thought I was only selected for regimental staff
because I was a woman. And I worried that they were right.

Were they looking at me like I was a token or was that my somewhat
paranoid imagination? I was really "token conscious", very worried about
being placed in a job I didn't deserve based upon my sex. I didn't want people talking about me, saying I only got the job because I was a female. Unless you have the credentials of Condaleeza Rice, you always have to wonder
if you would have gotten the job if you were a WASP. The shame of it is,
even Condaleeza probably wonders.

The S-4 is "Support" and that was me. So all I had to do was be myself.
And stay up late doing paperwork and worrying. If I'd been placed in a leadership position, I would have had to work on my aggressiveness and as-
sertiveness; I would have had to find some. But, as S-4, all I had to find were
sound trucks to make chapel in the field more fulfilling, find billets for the
soldiers supporting the weapons training, find tags for the barracks bags
that will be transported to and from the field.

"I like to go out and serve. It makes me feel humble."

—Letter to Steve, July, 1980

If you can't be with Mother Teresa in Calcutta, you may as well serve new cadets hot rations in the woods.

Not everyone agreed with my willingness to serve and accommodate. My assistant S-4 had a different philosophy. I vented to Steve in my daily letter. (This was before email, facebook and cell phones, so we wrote letters to each other daily, on paper with stamps, like in the Olden Days.)

"Yesterday, my assistant and I had an all-out argument, to include yelling and swearing on his part, due to our basic differences on philosophies of life. I cannot understand how anyone would not take a little effort to make someone else happy. I say, be nice to people even though it may take a little skin off your back. He says "Tough luck! If they don't follow the training schedule, and they cause trouble for you, too bad for them. Example: A company coming in early from the field wanted hot A's for lunch, instead of C's, so I went running around trying to get them the hot A's. This guy was not happy about it..."

Hot A's were just that: hot. The cooks in the mess hall dished their goods into "mermites", silver thermos jugs that could be transported easily. C's were C-rations, readily available cans of tasteless food, replaced in later years by Meals Ready to Eat (MRE's). Interestingly, my concept of service was in accordance with leadership doctrine; leaders are supposed to be selfless. But being selfless can lead to being walked on and the assistant S-4 was tired of being walked on. He obviously hadn't wanted to be a nun when he was younger. Those of us who had aspirations to feed the poor have a higher "Walk-on-me" threshold.

It was a summer of ups and downs. It had been that way since R-Day. I missed Steve and dove into work, spending the bits of free time we had with Linda and Meg. My running suffered and I intended to add the miles back into my day when the school year started, though I wasn't sure how much time I'd have then either. Cadet life, planning a wedding, and what cadet job would I have?

> **"Most of the trouble in the world is caused**
> **by people wanting to be important."**
>
> **—T.S. Eliot**

Another letter to Steve: "Major Kahara seems to think I ought to give Brigade S-4 a shot. I had a meeting with our new RTO (Regimental Tactical

Officer). I told him that I wanted to stay in the company. I told him that Activities Sergeant was an important job and I wanted it! He seemed like a good guy- but didn't seem to be real keen on me being F-2 Activities Sergeant. Tomorrow morning, they decide. I'll still get to sleep tonight…"

The RTO was the colonel responsible for the nine companies in second regiment, A-2 through I-2. The previous RTO, Colonel Solomon, had also been Commander of Beast and he'd interviewed me during Beast, along with all the other cadets in his regiment who were being considered for "outside the company" jobs. He asked me what I thought about being the Brigade S-4.

"Sir, I have to ask you," I began, "I have to ask if I'm just going to be a token."

What was I thinking? Did I think he'd say, "Well, yes, but you'd be an awfully cute one!"

Colonel Solomon paused. He told me my grades, my PE standing, my corps squad participation, everything was very competitive. I didn't say, "Yes, but do you realize I'm a Military Moron with No Leadership skills at all?"

I nodded to his kind words, but then I told him my feelings about being in the company.

We had a great group of people in F-2 and I wanted to spend my last year with them. I wanted to spend my last year with Linda as my roommate; I knew after graduation, we would be going our separate ways. I didn't want to leave the corps in the lurch, but I was pretty sure there were plenty of more competent, capable people than me who could adequately be in charge of the corp's laundry. I told him that I would love to plan F-2's parties, that this was vital to unit cohesiveness. Each company had an activities sergeant, fondly referred to as the party sergeant. This cadet planned social gatherings, parties, cook-outs, anything that "created unit cohesiveness", within reason, of course. He didn't tell me I was full of garbage and that party sergeant was a "sham" job (which would have been true). He listened and told me he'd make a recommendation based upon my input, my Tac's input, and Major Kahara's input.

The "Higher Authorities" decided I would spend the first half of my senior year in the brigade staff hallway, as one of the Assistant Brigade S-4s, and the second half of my firstie year, in F-2. This was a no-brainer. They selected Dena to be the S-4 and her talents put me to shame. A star woman (stars on the uniform collar meant you were in the top 5% academically in the class), she was also captain of the basketball team. I know when they listed our credentials in two columns; my "scoops out nice portions of mashed potatoes in the field to new cadets" couldn't come close to her "Rhodes Scholarship potential."

It fit me like a glove. I'd work my butt off first semester and have more time to plan the big wedding second semester. At the time, I didn't know that by January, it was too late to make wedding plans for the Royal Wedding to be held in May. Nor did I fully comprehend the very minor role I would play in this wedding anyway.

I was no longer worried about whether or not absence would make the heart grow fonder. The heart was fonder than ever. It was too fond. The brain would say, "Hey, you're a practical gal. Get a grip!" and the heart would say, "How many days until Labor Day weekend? I can't make it!" Meg, Brenda, and I had reservations on the same flight to Columbus, Georgia. We were all engaged to guys in the Class of '80 who were at the Infantry Basic Course; we were all in love, wishing our young lives away, counting down the days till graduation and our weddings.

Senior year: (*left to right*) Linda, Gail, Lori

thirteen

Firstie Year

*"If we had no winter, the spring
would not be so pleasant, if we
did not sometimes taste adversity,
prosperity would not be so welcome."*

—Anne Bradstreet

Whoever figured out time, was no mathematician. There may be eleven months between R-Day and Recognition; the same eleven months between the first day of firstie year and graduation, an equal number of dates on your calendar, marked with big X's, then ripped off. But plebe year creeps, like molasses, an electrical engineering lecture, the ninth month of a pregnancy. And firstie year zips by so quickly that if you're not paying attention, one morning you wake up and you're a second lieutenant, paying utility bills, and still not using a glass when you brush your teeth.

The first three years were filled with moments that made you just want to stand up and quit, to walk away and never come back. It was never ending, like a bad movie, that you keep saying you're going to get up and walk out of, but then there's a little funny scene and you stay, and then you say I'm out of here, this is awful, but then you think well, I paid for it, but it's not worth the $6.50, and you start to leave, but your friend says no, it will get better. You thought you'd be in the barracks forever, a permanent fixture,

153

like Ernie, the janitor with the emphysema cough who'd cleaned the toilets on the fifth floor of Central Barracks for about fifty years.

And then, you wake up one morning and it's September and you're a First Classman. Firstie means West Point ring, branch selection, and post selection. It means wearing your branch insignia on the collar of your class shirt, stenciling your foot locker with your name, then packing it up and sending it to your first Army post. And then you're in the Superintendent's Garden, crammed with people wearing fancy clothes, holding warm iced tea in plastic glasses, for the Graduation Reception with your parents and assorted relatives, listening to your grandmother say that you look like a Good Humor Ice Cream man in your starched, crisp white uniform.

First, the ring, the coveted West Point ring, the visible sign that yes, I am a member of the Long Grey Line. I wanted my ring to be pretty. Eagles, crests, flags, swords, helmets crowd the ring; it's not the easiest thing in the world to make simple and pretty. It's a man's ring. Some of the female cadets ordered miniatures, gift versions of the men's ring that mothers and wives have worn for years. I couldn't. I needed something that showed that I wasn't a mother or wife. I "hacked" through the obstacle course for four years; I low-crawled in the summer. I wouldn't say it aloud, but I thought it: I'm wearing a wedding band to show I'm a wife. I'm wearing a West Point ring to show I'm a graduate. I would have worn the thing if it were the size of a hula-hoop. I chose an opal; its pastel stone flashed just the right touch of femininity. I loved it. Still do.

Branch selection was harder. I was clueless. This would be the specialty area that I would serve in for a minimum of five years, maybe longer. We prioritized what branch we wanted in what order and then waited for the "higher authorities" to decide, based upon class rank and how many slots West Point had for each branch. My rank was just OK, a little over 100 out of 900. Linda's was lower so she'd have less choice. As an Army brat, she knew far more than I did about what each branch was all about, but all her knowledge was for naught since she'd be "ranked." Being "ranked" meant that you had no choice. You'd be placed in a branch that had slots that were not filled. If Linda wanted to go Engineer branch, but Engineer "went out" with the classmate who was ranked 450 in class, and Field Artillery (FA) had 350 slots and only 325 were filled and the other branches were all filled, the guys at the bottom of the class would be placed, "ranked", in FA to fill those slots. Field Artillery and Air Defense Artillery were the "ranked" branches that year. Linda figured she was going to be ranked so she learned all she could about both branches. She became an expert on Field Artillery, then surprised herself by not being ranked after all. She selected FA anyway.

We had been introduced, supposedly, to the branches when we were third classman at Camp Buckner. To me, it was like going into Baskin Robbins and peering through the frosty glass at thirty different flavors, with no time to read what the ingredients were or take a taste test. Oh, we did taste about fifteen scoops of Infantry; we BINGED on Infantry! But Quartermaster? Military Intelligence? Transportation? We didn't touch them. It was up to us to talk to officers and research the branches on our own.

I had spent my CTLT time as a Military Intelligence platoon leader and it was not a pleasant experience. No one in that unit asked for my opinion on the SALT II Treaty, nor did anyone approach me and ask me if I wanted to redefine national strategic objectives. I had assumed that my electives, all in the International Relations field, would prime me for MI. Rather, a good course at the post service station, learning how to fix jeeps, would have been more useful. I still had MI on my list, but after learning that I wasn't going to be on the National Security Counsel or wearing a cloak and dagger, I wasn't sure if I wanted it to be my first choice.

Quartermaster meant logistics. I'd done this during Beast, did OK in it, and it made the most sense. I enjoyed seeing things happen. I liked to serve people. We picked branches in early December, and until November, I was going Quartermaster.

As far as posts go, I had to go where Steve was going: Fort Ord, California. Not a bad deal. The problem was that when Steve selected Ft. Ord, he was choosing from Infantry, and since, at that time, Ft. Ord housed the 7th Infantry Division, there were a lot of Infantry slots available. Not the case from my branch. If I were lucky, there might be one Quartermaster or MI slot at Ord. They assured us that Joint Domicile, the Army program that tried to place active duty spouses together, would work, *if the needs of the Army were met.* I didn't like the sounds of that *if the needs of the Army were met.* From what I could see, the Army was pretty needy. We didn't choose posts until after Christmas, so I had plenty of time to worry about not being able to live with my husband.

✦ ✦ ✦ ✦

"People seem not to see that their
opinion of the world is also a
confession of their character."

—Ralph Waldo Emerson

I was supposed to have had it all together by firstie year, but I missed the boat completely when it came to character and friendship. There were two guys in F-2 who got in trouble. Both were caught smoking pot at parties off post. The disciplinary proceedings included a board in which the cadet in trouble was allowed to have character witnesses. We were a tight company and I knew these guys, both were hilarious, fun-loving, smart, but a bit on the wild side, which went with the charge. Both asked me to testify for them: the female on brigade staff, lots of stripes on the sleeve of her uniform. Just because they got caught doing drugs didn't mean they were stupid.

I stood before the officers conducting that board and told them that these guys both made a one-time mistake in judgment. I thought this single grave mistake did not reflect the potential of the individual as an officer. I cringe when I look in life's rear view mirror and hear myself talk about officership like I actually thought I knew something about it! After three and a half years at West Point, and only months away from being commissioned a second lieutenant, I still thought that West Point owed it to the "good guys."

Much later in life, I taught a course called *Officership* to yearlings, a two week class that focused on the tenets of being an Officer in the Army. Trent, a student in my class, told me that he had just figured out that not all of his friends who are good guys should be at West Point; that good guys sometimes need to be at other colleges. I was humbled listening to this kid. It took me years to figure that out.

**"A lot of people run a race to see who's the fastest.
I run to see who has the most guts."**

—Steve Prefontaine

I had to keep running. I still had vomit flashbacks from my cross-country experience, and besides, with the crop of new recruits in, I wouldn't make the team anyway. I had a flash of brilliance: I'd run with the Marathon Club. This great idea would allow me to run miles, far and slow. I didn't know much about it, but decided to show up for the try-outs, a six-mile run out to Round Pond and back.

Captain McNally showed up to watch the try-outs. They just don't make sponsors any nicer than that. He chatted with me as we stretched before the start, near the grey cement statue of Sylvanus Thayer, The Father Of The

Gail, on far right, marching with brigade staff. Fall 1980

Military Academy. He heard me talk to the Officer-in-Charge of the team, a blond haired major who held a clipboard near the start. I told Major Brown, shyly, embarrassed, that I wanted to try out and run with the team, but I'd never be able to run a marathon and I saw Captain McNally, overhearing, shaking his head and smiling. I was just being honest! The team trained for the Marine Corps Marathon, held the first Sunday in November, 26.2 miles, a solid 18 miles more than I'd ever run in my life. Major Brown listened to me, nodded, and told me to get over with the other cadets at the start, to run out to Round Pond for the try-outs and we'd talk about a marathon later. I finished the course in forty-two minutes, breaking no records, but one of the advantages of this Marathon Club idea of mine was that there were four slots for women and only three of us were trying out. Being a minority wasn't always a bad deal.

When I finished, Major Brown called me over.

"Now, what were you saying about not being able to run a marathon?"

I told him very honestly that I loved to run, but there was no way in the world I could run a full marathon. I was hoping that I could just train with the team. He grinned.

"You'll train with the team. But you'll also run the marathon."

Oozing with my usual overflowing levels of self-confidence, I shook my head, but didn't argue. After all, he was a Major. But he was very mistaken. I'd done a lot of things at West Point that I didn't think I'd be able to do, but I knew there was *no* possible way I could finish a marathon.

I had many needs. I needed to get good grades because I was a nerd at heart who would be drop dead disappointed in myself if I got a C. (And I did, so I know.) I needed quiet to study because I had the attention span of a gnat. I needed hours and hours to study because I was simple, forced to write reams of notes, memorizing, quizzing myself and memorizing some more. I used every spare moment to get those hours in. Shining shoes, sitting on the hopper, even running. To get the quiet, I went to the library or over to Linda's room every night and to get the sleep, I was in bed by taps, midnight was a late night.

The cadets on Brigade Staff didn't have these needs. When they mistakenly selected me to live in that hallway, they forgot to ask if I needed study or sleep. The other cadets on brigade staff were light years smarter than me and really were very nice about it. Brigade staff can develop an elitist attitude, a "we're the best and the brightest" aura. Not these guys.

But I missed Steve. I missed Linda. I got tired of laundry not being picked up in the sallyports and tired of telling other cadets to get those racks of dress grey out of there. I lived for phone calls to Steve and running. I was a woman obsessed. With many things. Studying, running and still, eating. I weighed ninety-five pounds but was obsessed with what I put in my body for food. My letters to Steve were full of what I ate and if I was "good" eating that day. I was developing lousy eating habits. On Sundays, I'd down a box of granola cereal—that's it for the day. Not much variety in that diet and tough on the roommate as well. I had started eating some fats; I knew that the long miles we put in on the marathon team would negate any fat calories I consumed and on crumb cake days in the mess hall, I'd slice the tops off and eat plates of crumb topping, but still added nothing to my pathetic frame.

I had no idea I was so pitifully thin. People tried to tell me, but I didn't listen. Linda, concerned, told me all the time. Mostly I just got wise cracks. Dr. Peterson, the Dragon Lady in the Department of Physical Education, called me in to her office, made me sit down, leaned over her desk, looked at me anxiously.

"You're so thin," she said, "Too thin. You're doing well in PE so I don't think you're weak because of your weight, but you really ought to weigh more. I recommend that you take some extra calories in; try having those instant drink mixes just for the caloric intake. You're burning up more than you're putting in every day."

What a response I had.

"I'll be honest with you, Ma'am," I replied. "I don't want to gain weight and have to go mess with those tailors altering all my uniforms. I don't have time for that. I've never been big and I feel fine."

Always polite, I thanked her for her time and concern.

Women don't see what's really in the mirror. It's a genetic defect we're born with. But I look back now at pictures of how thin I was then, and am appalled. I knew I was thin, but figured I was the same thin I was in high school. I'd gone way past that thin, though. I was skin and bones.

My weight ended up being the least of my health concerns. Who would have thought that I'd fail the commissioning exam?

Every first classman took a medical exam during firstie year. Similar to the medical that was required to obtain an appointment to West Point, passing this exam was required before being commissioned as a second lieutenant in the Army. I arrived at the exam skinny, dumb and happy. I wasn't worried. I hadn't been in the hospital since my fat foot incident plebe year. I never got sick.

The Tac called me down to his office.

Unfit to be commissioned, read the paperwork.

"You'll get a degree, the bachelor of science in general engineering, like everyone else," he told me. "But you won't get a commission."

He dropped this ton of bricks on me calmly, matter of factly. I thought *They had to have made a mistake.* A hearing problem! A "Severe" Hearing Problem! I told the Tac that Linda mumbled and I didn't hear in lectures, but no one did, did they?

Hank had been transferred to another post. This was our new Tac, Major Fishowitz, a nice guy, a non-grad, puffy with a pipe; he reminded me of Fred MacMurray on My Three Sons.

"It's not a bad deal. You'll get a West Point diploma, but owe the Army no time at all. You could go anywhere, do anything. Think about it."

I left his office in a daze. It was October. If I wanted to fight the finding, I'd have to be boarded medically. They'd convene a medical board and I'd have to write arguments and ask people to testify for me, recommending that I be commissioned. Or else, I could just take this and run. I would graduate. I would have a diploma to frame and hang on the wall. I would toss my hat up in the air, but then I wouldn't change into my green Class A uniform. I wouldn't raise my hand and swear to defend the constitution of the United States of America.

The Tac told me to return the next day with my decision.

"The race goes not always to the swiftest...
but to those who keep on running."

—Annonymous

You just can't have it all. I loved the long runs the marathon team did, but I missed the girls on the cross-country team. The guys on the marathon team were too quick for me; the girls were just a bit slower. I ended up trying to hang with the guys for as long as I could, usually not long. I knew it was making me a better runner, but I prefer gossip to speed.

Major Brown ran with me one practice.

"Are you still convinced you can't do a marathon?"

I didn't skip a beat.

"Yes, Sir," I replied. Put that self-confidence in a thimble and then fill it, jump in and have enough room left over to take a bath!

He told me that he was going to run Marine Corps with me. He had already qualified for Boston and wanted to make sure I did. My eyes popped open. First, no way could I qualify for Boston. I'd be lucky if I finished the thing without keeling over. Second, what a nice thing for this man to do.

The prestigious Boston marathon requires you to "qualify" by running a specified time in another marathon. The cadets on the marathon team train for the Marine Corps marathon in hopes of qualifying for Boston and running infamous Heartbreak Hill the next April. For me to qualify, I had to run Marine Corps in less than 3:20 (3 hours 20 minutes). No way, I thought. I honestly thought that I'd be lucky to even finish the marathon, never mind run it at a sub-eight-minute mile pace. It wasn't as if I was coming from an over-zealous athletic background. Being kicked off intramural volleyball was not that long ago.

It was November 4, 1980, and I was scared to death, freezing cold and thinking that I might throw up. I wore my worn, white with red trim, Boston Red Sox T-shirt. My parents drove down and stayed with Aunt Mary who lived outside D.C. and I looked through the crowds mobbing the streets along the route to try to find them. Mrs. Brown, so sweet, was all over the course. Her husband was a regular marathoner, so she had long ago mastered the art of marathon spectatorship and she dashed from spot to spot, mile 2 to mile 6 to mile 14. I waved and smiled.

I felt good. I thought that I'd just keep going until I dropped. Major Brown knew how ugly that drop could be and was worried that we were going too fast. Before the race, he had pinned a tiny pace chart to his shorts. He knew exactly what time we should be at what mile to meet that magic time of 3:20. At mile 15, he told me we were ahead of schedule. Maybe we should slow down? Can't, Sir, I told him. I feel good. He wanted me to take water at the water stops. Can't, Sir, I told him. I feel good. I didn't want to mess up my stomach. He was worried. I didn't look at him, just kept looking ahead. I could tell he wanted me to stick to the pace chart, to slow down a little, but he let me go. His experience told him that I would surely dehydrate and he'd be stuck with me in a medic tent for hours. He must have figured by mile 23, I'd be dead on the side of the road. Our longest training run was twenty miles. Anything over that was in unmarked territory.

My very small brain was doing the running. I had mastered physical tasks at West Point through sheer determination and did the same for the marathon. We crossed the finish line in 3:08, a feeling that can only be compared to childbirth. I was the first female cadet to qualify for the Boston Marathon. This meant a lot to my mother and father, who didn't end up seeing me once the entire race and were worried sick when they saw me afterward, legs and stomach cramping, barely moving, but really, I was only in the second class to try to qualify and there weren't a truckload of women trying.

I never kept in touch with Major Brown. I heard years later that he'd made General. He'll always be Major Brown to me; the man who believed in me; the man who opened the door to marathoning and pushed me through.

"Keep true to the dreams of thy youth."

—Johann von Schiller

I returned to West Point after the marathon to my medical board. It was held that same week. An hour after the Tac had told me that I was unfit for commissioning; I'd gone back in to see him. I told him I didn't need the night to think it over. I wanted to fight the finding and receive a commission.

How ironic this was! There I was, a young girl who went to West Point for West Point, for the challenges of the college itself, certainly not for the Army afterward, an unknown that I never thought about. I never jumped into anything that was military, or even green, with both feet. *I* wouldn't want to be stuck behind enemy lines with *me*! Now faced with an option to receive a Bachelor of Science degree in General Engineering from West Point, free, no charge, and skip the whole Army thing, I chose, with not a touch of hesitation, to go the Army route.

Why? I had bitten hard and been hooked by the Duty, Honor, Country line. I bought it, hook, line and sinker. I wanted to be a part of it.

The board was held on the fifth floor of Washington Hall, up above the mess hall, after school. It was raining outside, cold and dreary. Captain Mc-Nally gave statements to the board, as did Major Fishowitz and Major Perry, a physical education instructor who worked with my company. I was outside in the hallway when they spoke about me. I wasn't allowed to hear what they had to say. They finally called me. I had memorized my statement, but my heart did the talking. I told the board that I should be commissioned; I didn't think I had a hearing problem; it hadn't affected me in my day-to-day life. I told the board that I had worked hard to become an officer in the Army; that I thought I could do it well. When I finished, I was shaking. An officer told me to go back out in the hall and wait. They would give me their findings after they deliberated.

I watched the rain hit the side of the windows and waited, shivering. It was incredible, I thought. My ears were fine. I couldn't believe this was happening.

One of the officers came out and got me. I stood at attention when the president of the board told me they had reached a decision.

I could even go Combat Arms, they told me.

The doctor couldn't hold back. He told me, as the rest of the board members sat quietly and listened, that he did not agree with the decision of the board. He wanted me to know, he said, that I was unfit to be commissioned. I had what he called genetic susceptibility to noise exposure; that I had suffered irreversible nerve damage, probably at Buckner firing the live light anti-tank weapon. My ears would never get better, he said. They would only get worse.

I kept blinking back tears. I felt like crying. The doctor's harsh words stung and scared me, but I didn't believe him. I was going to be commissioned and my ears were just fine.

I learned very quickly after graduation that the doctor had been right. I got my first hearing aid in 1982 and my second in 1984 and have been wearing two ever since. Twenty five years after graduation, I have 25% speech discrimination; I hear and understand one out of four words spoken to me. I wish I hadn't worn my ear plugs so loosely at Camp Buckner.

The phone rang in my room one night after dinner. It was Major Madison, the nice French teacher who once told me I had the worst pronunciation he'd ever heard in his life. He wanted to congratulate me on the marathon, and then we chatted some. He asked me about branches and I told him I was thinking Quartermaster. He was a Military Intelligence officer, he told me, a 35, tactical intelligence officer, and why didn't I come over some night for dinner and he could tell me about it. Free dinner. Nice guy. I'm up for learning more. Meg had been on me to go MI. She was convinced it was a great branch; her dad was an active duty MI colonel. She'd told me I shouldn't judge the whole branch on one lousy platoon and I knew she was right. I figured I should listen to Major Madison's guidance. We set a date for dinner.

Ring Banquet, firstie year: (*left to right*) Lori, Gail, Linda

fourteen

At the End of that Path

*"A friend is someone who thinks you're a good
egg even though you're slightly cracked."*

—Bernard Meltzer

Halfway there. Christmas leave. I broke my mother's heart and didn't go home for Christmas. I flew to California to spend time with Steve. I felt equal amounts of guilt and happiness: Guilt for not being home; happiness for being with Steve.

I learned over that Christmas vacation how love masks reality. Steve rented a one bedroom apartment in Pacific Grove, a quaint town of old hippies, artists, and beach bums. It was lovely, really. The reality, though, was that in his apartment, there was no food in the refrigerator and the freezer door wouldn't shut because of ice build-up. The toilet and tub had never been cleaned; he thought the water cleaned the toilet when you flushed; the shower water cleaned it as you bathed. The television was on a TV table, one foot away from his chair, so he could change channels with his bare toe, this, before the days of remote control. There were BB gun holes in the front door through the X of the EXIT sign. Sadly, I saw none of this because of the Love factor. Love masks reality. I spent the week staring at him googly-eyed, smiling and humming happily. Being in Love is like being a Moonie. Scary.

165

Driving through the gates at West Point after Christmas vacation always makes your stomach feel nauseous. Even firstie year, when you only have five months left, that dread, that depression, that dismal shroud of gloom filled the front seat of the car. At least I'd be moving back to the fifth floor of Central Barracks, leaving the Brigade Staff hallway and back to F-2. The Tac listened to our requests and Linda and I were assigned as roommates again. We'd come in together plebe year and we'd go out together as second lieutenants. Her friendship, and that of the guys in F-2, had made the four years bearable and I knew it. We picked our branches. We got post assignments. The light at the end of that tunnel was getting brighter and brighter.

I picked Military Intelligence. I don't know why. Meg was going, the Basic Course was not long (I was in a rush to get to Ft. Ord); and, I still harbored dreams of being asked my thoughts on foreign policy. I was ranked third in MI. That meant there were two guys ahead of me who could pick Ft. Ord and force me to rely totally upon Joint Domicile. I had no faith in the system and did not believe for a minute that Joint Domicile cared about me living with my husband. I talked to both of the guys who were ahead of me. Al wanted Hawaii and Matt wanted Ft. Lewis. I was set! Matt, small world, was the cute kid I was paired up with in that PAE held long ago in the gym at Ft. Devens; he was a good friend, like a brother.

The night of the post selection, we entered the large room in Washington Hall. All the MI cadets were in one room. The entire First Class selected their posts the same night. I was early. Nerds usually are. Matt was there early, too, and he came over to me. He looked worried. He hesitated. Oh, oh, I thought, This is not good.

Matt paused and looked down at his shoes. This was not good. Finally, he said, apologetically, "Gail, I'm so sorry…but I want to go to Ft. Ord."

I gawked. I'm sure my mouth hung open and my eyes popped wide. He was guiltily rambling now.

"I've wanted Ft. Ord but didn't want to take it from you because I know you wanted it to be with Steve. But I've been talking to people and they tell me that you'll get it automatically once you get married."

I couldn't talk. I was afraid I was going to cry. Matt had a lot more faith in the Army than I did. But I felt bad for him. He was smart, and worked hard; he should have been able to pick the post he wanted.

I managed to tell him no problem, I understood, no big deal.

Meg came in. I couldn't tell her. I was afraid I was going to cry. I'd still only cried one time in front of another cadet, at Camp Buckner when I found out I didn't get that Recondo patch. I finally told Meg. She told me not to worry. It

would work out. Mark had gone Aviation and wouldn't know where he'd be going after flight school. They hoped to be stationed together at Ft. Campbell, but
she was in the same boat I was: dependent upon Joint Domicile.

They flashed the posts that were available up on an overhead and called
us out, by rank in the branch, and asked us what post we wanted. Al stood
up when they called him and picked Hawaii. Matt stood up and said Ft. Ord.
He didn't sound happy about it; I knew he felt bad. There was a groan in the
room; the other ten MI cadets all knew that I wanted it. It was my turn next.
There were three Ft. Campbell slots and if I picked it, there would still be
one for Meg. My brother Paul was there. I figured if I couldn't live with my
husband, I could live with Paul and his wife, Pattie. I said "Fort Campbell",
waited for the others to draw and wandered back to the company. The Zoo
was wild. Lori was going to Italy, Linda was going to Germany. Barry was
going to Alaska, Brian was going to Ft. Ord. Ian asked me, innocently, well,
Gail, what'd you get? I cried. Poor Ian didn't know why I fell apart. It was the
second and final time in my cadet career that I cried in front of someone.

I just had to hope Joint Domicile would do its trick.

✦ ✦ ✦ ✦

Nothing can ruin a pretty good mother-daughter relationship faster than
planning a wedding. Take a stubborn, independent daughter with no time
and a mother who didn't have a real wedding forty years earlier. You'll get a
mother getting married and the daughter walking down the aisle.

My mother had a train ticket, December 1942. By herself, she left South
Station for South Dakota to marry my father before he shipped out to the
Pacific during the big one, WWII. She never had a real wedding, no brides-
maids, no flowers, no reception with an Irish band and chicken breast and
potatoes au gratin. Until I got married.

Really, it worked out for me. Once I got it in my head that it was out of
my hands, I was relieved. My brain was focused only on Graduation/Living
with Steve. Getting married was just something in between. I would have
been happy to ask Father Berube, our parish priest, to meet us at the church
one night. We'd treat him to McDonald's after. I was not into the whole expense and drama of the wedding day. It just wasn't me.

✦ ✦ ✦ ✦

I didn't see Steve between Christmas and Graduation. He went to the
field during spring break and I went home to nod my head yes to whatever

my mother said about the wedding. She'd orchestrated everything from who would read what reading in mass to where we'd stand in the receiving line. Everything was done. We were set. I just had to show up.

I didn't run the Boston Marathon. I listened to the voices telling me not to do it and I regretted it for years. My mother was vehemently opposed to me running a marathon a month and a half before my wedding.

"You'll end up coming down the aisle in a wheelchair!"

You have to understand life in the '70s; she had never seen me sweat before in my life. The first time my parents saw me exerting myself was at a cross-country meet at West Point. Despite my efforts to find a tree and hide behind it, my mother happened to catch me dry-heaving at the finish line.

"Can't you slow down, honey? The trees are just beautiful. All the leaves are changing! Can't you slow down and enjoy the scenery?"

Mothers. You have to love them.

After the Marine Corps marathon, back at my Aunt Mary's house, she made me go weigh myself. It wasn't pretty. I weighed eighty-five pounds and she saw the scale. I tried to tell her it was water weight, it would be back by the time I ate my first meal. I looked lousy, I felt lousy and I crawled, like anyone does, after a marathon. She feared that I'd lose more weight and get hurt if I ran Boston. I regretted not running it for years. Twenty-one years, to be exact.

They were all coming for Graduation week. Steve took two weeks leave and flew in from Ft. Ord. Mom and Dad, Garrett, my oldest brother whom I hadn't seen in four years, and his new Native American Indian wife, as in fresh off the reservation, flew in from Arizona. Paul and a very pregnant wife Pattie drove up from Ft. Campbell. Fred, his girlfriend, also Gail, and Aunt Rita and Uncle Gerard drove up with my parents. This must be what they call a Chinese Fire Drill, getting all these relatives to the right hall for the right function at the right time, hope everyone was having a good time. Graduation week, though less physically demanding, ranks up there with Beast Barracks as far as stress goes. Then throw the Royal Wedding in, three days later, back home in Massachusetts. Can you say Insane Asylum?

Ronald Reagan spoke, but I didn't listen. I was overwhelmed. Disbelief. I'm graduating from West Point? Incredible joy. I'm going to live with Steve. Sadness. I'm going to miss Linda, Meg, the McNally's, F-2. And then more Disbelief. I cannot believe that I did this.

I read about it years later in a women's magazine. I had an anxiety attack in line, waiting to march up and receive that diploma from the commandant of cadets. I wanted to run, just get out of there. I was suddenly petrified, scared to death.

It passed.

I walked up onto the stage. I saluted, shook General Franklin's hand, took the diploma and returned to my seat. Everyone was hugging. I looked for Linda; it was alphabetical and she was on her way up to the podium. I searched for Steve, for my parents in the stands. We sang the Alma Mater. We uncovered, took our white caps off our heads. We threw them up, high, white specks of freedom, of pride, of accomplishment against the blue sky.

It was finally over. I'd still be back where those roads diverged if it hadn't been for family, mentors, friends, an old nun's vote of confidence. Their unconditional support shaded me along the way; but my own determination drove me down that path, a path less traveled. I stumbled, fell, got up, ran, and stumbled again. But I finally got there.

I'd like to think I left footprints on the path, made it easier for others to travel this route. But that would be vain. The mark I left on West Point is a mere speck, like that white cap amongst hundreds thrown up in the air, compared to the mark it left on me. It does that to people. And that has made all the difference.

At Class of 1981's 25th reunion in 2006: (*left to right*) Teesa, Gail, Linda, Liz

The "Archies" at the 25th reunion: (*left to right*) Mike, Patty, Gail, Jimmy.

fifteen

Where They Are Today

Patty, Mike, Jimmy from Archbishop Williams High: Patty and Dan have been married for twenty-eight years, have four kids and live in Dallas, Texas. Mike got out of the Army after five years, and lives in Albuquerque with wife Nicki and son Michael. Jimmy is married with three kids, an Army Aviator, and a Brigadier General.

Meg and Brenda: Both married the lieutenants we flew to visit on Labor Day. We are all still married, somehow, to our cadet-dates. Brenda and Mike's son, Michael, graduated in the Class of 2005 and was the first West Point graduate whose parents were both West Point graduates. Brenda is the first female graduate wife of the Commandant of Cadets at West Point. Meg and Mark's daughter, Megan, graduated in the Class of 2006. Megan was the first female graduate whose parents were both graduates.

Teesa and Liz: In August 2007, the three of us joined the "old graduates" who marched back from their end of summer bivouac with the Class of 2011. Old F-2 friends are friends for life.

F-2 Class of 1981: Haven't changed a bit and that's a good thing. Hairlines and guts have been altered, but all else remains the same, to include maturity level. I credit my positive four year experience to Linda and F-2.

Jeff and Carolyn McNally: Jeff remains at West Point, buried in the cemetery after succumbing to a long battle with cancer, in 1996. He touched hundreds of cadets and I'm grateful I was one of them. Carolyn raised their daughter Sara and still teaches me, without trying.

Linda: Met and married a classmate when they were stationed together as lieutenants in Germany. Linda got out of the Army after eight years to raise their two girls. Her oldest daughter graduated from the Air Force Academy. We e-mail, talk, send birthday and Christmas gifts. She still tells corny jokes and I still laugh.

Kim and Sharon: Both still live within ten miles of Robinson Avenue. They are the sisters I never had.

My Parents: Have both died. I miss them every day.

Brother Paul: Retired after twenty years in the Army, works for the State Department fighting drugs, which is as close to being a cowboy as he can get. He remains my idol.

Brother Fred: An English teacher and writer who edited this story, still goes by Fred, still leans back in his chair.

Steve: Living proof that a mediocre cadet career does not necessarily predict mediocrity in the Army. After twenty-seven years in the Army, he retired after commanding an aviation brigade. He still makes me laugh. My best friend and father of our four great kids.

Three days after Gail's graduation, she and Steve marry at St. Francis of Assisi Church, Braintree, Massachusetts. Saber bearers: (*from bottom left*) Mike McGrath, Bill Buckley, Charlie Gleichenhaus (brother Paul's West Point roommate); (*from bottom right*) Jim McConville, Wayne Young, brother Paul. May 30, 1981

Me: We have four children (*see photo below*): Steve, 23, West Point Class of 2009; Chris, 22, a teacher; Tim, 20, West Point Class of 2011; and Maria, a high school senior. I've served as a West Point Admissions field force member since 1993. From 2000-02, when my husband was stationed at West Point, I ran with the Women's Marathon team, and in April 2002, with the team, I finally ran Boston. Amazingly, the 3:08 I ran in 1980 stands as the female cadet marathon record at West Point. I remain grateful for the opportunity that I was given in 1977 to take a path less traveled. My life has been what it is because I took that path. I'm so glad that I did.

The Long Gray Line continues: Steve, Jr (*third from left*) graduates in 2009. "Although the admittance of women to West Point broke tradition, it built new ones, an unintended consequence that will ultimately increase and strengthen that line of gray."

acknowledgments

I only have this story to tell thanks to:

-My parents who didn't let their real and valid concerns close the door on my dreams and who were always there for me;

-My family who not only gave me the idea (Thanks, Paul), but also gave me a bit of sarcasm, my nose and all those other O'Sullivan-McGonagle traits that make me who I am;

-Robinson Avenue, for a childhood that all children deserve;

-My classmates in '81, SAO;

-And especially to '81 in F-2, for your friendship.

So many people encouraged me to write this story. My brothers, mother-in-law, sister-in-law, friends, graduates, parents of candidates and cadets. Thanks to all.

Special thanks to our four great kids: Steve, Chris, Tim and Maria.

And there's one person who is central to my story and has spent twenty-six years trying to convince me to write it. He encouraged; he proofread; he wouldn't let me give up. My husband, my best friend, has supported me in whatever I have done since the first day we met in Old South barracks. (I still say he had gym shorts on.) This story would be on my hard drive and would not have this happy ending…if it weren't for him.

B
DWYER

Dwyer, Gail
O'Sullivan.

Tough as nails.

MARY JACOBS LIBRARY
64 WASHINGTON ST.
ROCKY HILL, NJ 08553

9/09

Printed in the United States
221043BV00005B/2/P

9 781555 716639